Fishing Flies

An Illustrated Album

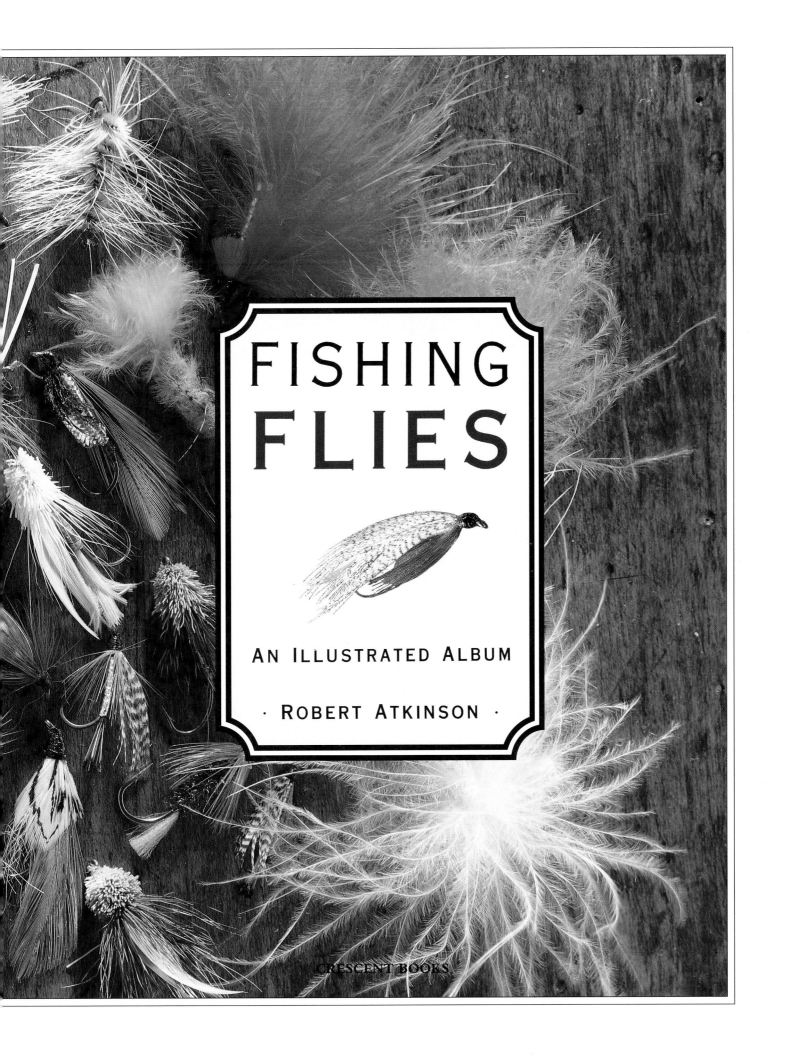

FISHING
FLIES

AN ILLUSTRATED ALBUM

· ROBERT ATKINSON ·

CRESCENT BOOKS

FISHING FLIES WAS FIRST PUBLISHED BY HC BLOSSOM
BOOKS, 6 WARREN MEWS, LONDON W1P 5DJ ENGLAND

COPYRIGHT © 1991 HC BLOSSOM

THIS 1991 EDITION PUBLISHED BY CRESCENT BOOKS,
DISTRIBUTED BY OUTLET BOOK COMPANY, INC.
A RANDOM HOUSE COMPANY, 225 PARK AVENUE SOUTH,
NEW YORK, NEW YORK 10003

PRINTED AND BOUND IN HONG KONG

ISBN 0-517-05416-7

8 7 6 5 4 3 2 1

Contents

INTRODUCTION 7
DRY FLIES 17
WET FLIES 51
NYMPHS – RIVER TROUT 61
LURES – RIVER TROUT 85
TEAL SERIES – SEA TROUT 107
RARE FEATHERS – SALMON 111
FANCY PATTERNS 117
LEECHES 121
INDEX 126

Introduction

Fly-fishing can be an idle pastime, a serious hobby or a full-blown sport – depending on the passion with which it is embraced. The coarse-fisherman's experience may not extend beyond the odd cast to a lake trout to keep himself occupied during the close-season of his own sport, whereas another will invest thousands to catch the king of gamefish, the salmon. Yet both have one thing in common – they will be using a *fly*, like as not constructed from fur, feather and, nowadays, plastic to tempt the quarry.

The layman may be excused for believing that the adornment of a hook with such materials is merely an affectation of the modern age, perhaps conjuring up images of country gentlemen casting silken lines upon the gentle waters of English chalkstreams or tweeded ghillies humouring salmon fishers in Scotland. He would, in fact, be wrong on two counts, for the practice is neither an affectation nor of recent origin.

The use of an artificial fly has several advantages, not the least of which is practicality. Consider the alternative: First Catch Your Fly. Immediately the tranquillity of the river bank is shattered by hordes of stomping fishermen thrashing the air with butterfly nets. Having caught an insect, our angler proceeds with the delicate and exasperating task of attaching the creature (still alive) to a hook. This is by no means easy, for insects have a policy of non-cooperation with the world in general and *Homo sapiens* in particular; but let us give man the benefit of the doubt and a little strong glue.

It is now time to cast (very gently or the insect will part company with the hook) to a likely fish which, seeing a creature mounted on a skewer, decides it will make a tasty meal. In due course our angler lands his fish. Unfortunately, fish possess sharp teeth and strong jaws, a combination which has a similar effect on the soft-bodied insect to a car travelling at speed, so it is time for the butterfly net again. And at the end of the day, there is little point in keeping the survivors, for insects are very short-lived. A whole new sport thus develops: fly-catching. Commercial fly-breeding proliferates alongside kindly folk determined to abolish cruelty to insects. Clearly this would not work. Accordingly, human ingenuity through the centuries has made use of everyday materials to imitate these creatures; and these artificial creations are collectively called *flies*.

Why do these scraps of fur and feather catch fish? Quite simply, freshwater fish rely on aquatic creatures to form the mainstay of their diet. Depending on the type of water and its location, a fish would normally expect to see on the menu aquatic insects, their larvae or pupae, small crustaceans, tiny fish (called *fry*), land-borne insects (terrestrials), and even frogs. Whereas most species of fish subject to the angler's attention may be caught *on the fly*, one group in particular lends itself admirably to the method: gamefish – those which offer a combination of sport and meal – notably salmon, trout, char and grayling.

The modern fly-tyer will therefore *dress* flies (for that is how the process of making them is described) in the pursuit of sport. But that has not always been the case. There is evidence that man has utilised this method for literally thousands of years – Macedonians, Egyptians, Greeks and Romans have all left their mark – but uncertainty exists as to whether the use of the artificial arose for sporting or more practical reasons.

The first written evidence of the subject in English is *The Treatysse of Fysshynge With an Angle,* published in 1496. Tradition ascribes this book to Dame Juliana Berners, Abbess of Sopwell near St Albans in Hertfordshire; but modern research by the eminent historian and fly-fisher Jack Heddon bestows the honour on an anonymous author whose writings were published in London by the printer Wynkyn de Worde, a former employee of William Caxton. Whatever the truth, this tells us more about the history of publishing than the use of the fly in angling, for we know that the North American Indians used bone hooks dressed with fur and feather long before that. Which takes us back to the argument about affectation.

Although the *Treatysse* formed part of a more extensive work on hunting, falconry and fishing

for the medieval gentry who enjoyed their sport much as we do today, the American Indian was doubtless more preoccupied with filling his stomach than having fun. He used the fly for one simple reason – it was the most efficient method of catching fish. His bait could be utilised time and time again, and when he had finished, it slipped neatly into the pocket (or its equivalent), ready for another day. Try doing that with a maggot.

In the present age of invention, we are accustomed to radical change in our everyday lives, but such has not always been the case. Early man may well have imitated the natural food diet of fish in order to catch his dinner. That method would then have been adopted by professional fishermen to earn their living, as some do to this day. Another man with more time on his hands might have emulated that technique for purposes of sport. Be that as it may, the method has evolved, and so have the artificial flies associated with it – certainly over the past

few centuries – from the twelve mentioned in the *Treatysse* to the hundreds, if not thousands, available today. This evolution will be evident as we examine specific patterns in due course, but first, in order to appreciate the artificial copy, we have to understand something about the living creatures. The fly-fishing enthusiast, in particular, needs some knowledge of entomology, the study of insects, if he is to attempt a successful imitation of a natural species.

The eggs of aquatic insects are either laid in or on the water to rest on the river or lake bed, although in some instances they are attached to underwater plants. The eggs hatch into larvae or nymphs, depending on the species, and either swim freely, crawl or burrow as they feed and grow.

During this period of their lives, which may last for two years or more, they are the very bread and butter of predatory fish and must protect themselves as best they can. Eventually the survivors respond to nature's call and climb, stagger or swim to the water's surface or bank to hatch into winged insects. This is an important moment, in that the infant now abandons its protective natural cover to journey through open water to the surface. That in itself is a problem, for the effect of air pressure creates a meniscus, or membrane, on the water surface, rather like a skin on soup. This meniscus presents a barrier to anything as puny as the emerging insect, which hangs from the underside of the surface before struggling through. Once this is achieved, the youthful insect pauses to allow the sun to dry its wings sufficiently to fly, for the troublesome barrier has now become the ice rink on which it may rest.

If the insect's earlier life was fraught with dangers, that was as nothing by comparison to this journey, because hungry fish are lurking for just such an opportunity. During its ascent, struggling beneath the surface film or on the surface itself, the insect is an easy meal; the fish may be smaller than a shark but it possesses exactly the same instincts. Yet some insects do survive and fly off to rest in the bankside vegetation, awaiting final transformation into adulthood. This happens very quickly and the adult, or *imago*, dressed in sparkling hues that are only truly appreciated by another of its kind, flies off towards courtship and inevitable mating. Once the deed is done, the male leaves the scene like a wayward husband; of no further use to spouse or fish (and consequently anglers), it dies, leaving procreation to the female. She returns to the water, laying her eggs in the surface film or crawling down into the vegetation, depending on species. Then, in a scene that would do justice to a theatrical tragedy, her job done, the female falls exhausted upon the water which gave her life, and with wings spread-eagled is carried along by the current, helpless prey once again to the remorseless fish.

The angler attempts to reproduce the scenario of this life-cycle with an artificial and gives each stage a name. The crawling baby is a *nymph*, the ascending infant is an *emerger*, the youngster on the surface is a *dun*, the breeding adult is a *spinner*, and the dying adult, appropriately, a *spent spinner*. His artificial patterns are similarly divided: the nymphal stage is represented by nymph patterns, wet flies (so called because they are fished beneath the surface) or lures, while the duns, spinners and spent spinners are imitated by dry flies, fished on the surface. However, there are no hard and fast rules, and sometimes a wet or dry, sometimes called a *damp*, may be fished in the surface film.

The nature and function of the lure is a somewhat controversial issue. It is certainly effective, but we do not really know why it works so well. It may be that the fish believes it to be a food form, such as a larva or small fish which forms part of its normal diet. Alternatively, it may ignore its standard type of sustenance and decide to take a bite anyway. Or it may simply attack as a result of fear, curiosity or aggressiveness.

The fly-tyer may faithfully reproduce the natural – this he calls the *exact imitation*. Given a stretch of water, his selection of artificial must take account of season, location and time of day

when deciding not only which natural to reproduce but also the actual stage in that natural's life-cycle. Having made a choice, he must then allow it to move in the manner of that natural. This method presupposes a specific preference on the part of the fish.

Alternatively, working on the belief that a fish is not always particular about its diet, and is guided by instinct rather than what we commonly understand as intelligence, the fly-tyer may decide simply to copy the salient features of an insect, creating a so-called *general pattern*, designed along quite logical lines. So the finished fly looks sufficiently like an insect or bug to fool the fish. This type of pattern is especially valuable on fast-flowing rivers or in deep, dark waters where the fish has little opportunity for close scrutiny.

The possibility that the fish reacts as it does from fear or natural aggressiveness has little to do with food, but focuses on instincts of self-preservation. To survive the attentions of a predator, creatures in the wild must possess a highly efficient defence mechanism. Fish have a remarkable turn of speed, good eyesight and well developed senses of taste, touch and smell. They also boast sharp teeth and powerful jaws which are essential for investigation, feeding and defence. If an unusual item is passed rapidly across a fish's line of vision, it will frequently strike and grasp the object in the only way it can: with its mouth. This is the principle of the lure, usually a fanciful, non-representational object, but of great importance to the salmon fisherman.

The salmon spends its infancy in the river of its birth before journeying seawards to feed in richer pastures. When it is ready – and only a salmon knows when that is – it travels back to this same river to breed. The journey is long and arduous: bouts of enormous energy expenditure to overcome the strong river current and natural obstacles are interspersed with periods of rest in small pools. It is believed to navigate by sense of smell, each river having a unique odour; and as far as is known, it takes no food after leaving saltwater, relying instead on energy stored in the body tissues. So nobody knows for certain why

salmon should be caught in freshwater on fly or lure, but theories abound. Perhaps it is a response to a food item triggered by memories of feeding in the ocean; or it may be a manifestation of the aggressive instinct which is particularly pronounced in the breeding season – salmon do get hungry and will feed if the opportunity occurs. Probably there is some truth in all the various arguments advanced. Whatever the truth, the methods of the salmon angler are legion.

Having briefly summarised the various fly-tying styles, it is worth looking at the materials used in their manufacture. First and foremost is the hook, the foundation stone of the fly. The lowly hook, in fact, is worthy of a book to itself, for over the centuries a myriad designs, shapes and sizes have been developed for different styles of fishing. Ancient man used hooks fashioned from bone, a material he found sufficiently strong and sharp, yet flexible enough for a barb to be carved at the point to prevent the hook slipping out. A hand-made bone hook would certainly have been a tool of considerable value, and the introduction of readily available metal hooks must in some way have debased the article's worth, but it did enable the angler to concentrate on his dressings. Attaching the hook to the line, however, was still a laborious task: the shank would be *whipped* with gut, the angler's *cast*, which in turn was affixed to a line of woven horse's tail; and it was not yet possible to change patterns rapidly to suit prevailing conditions. The introduction of the eyed hook, and subsequent mechanical production in the latter part of the nineteenth century, was a truly significant step forward: unencumbered by his reluctance to change hooks, the fly-fisher would seek patterns far more varied than ever used previously, thus ensuring the further development of the art.

Today there exists a wide variety of strong, astonishingly sharp and perfectly tempered hooks, in a range of weights and sizes to satisfy every eventuality. And with an increasing awareness of the need to conserve native stock, we are finally losing the barb. That which was so important to the hunter is now anathema to the sportsman; he requires a hook which makes it possible for a wild fish to be easily released, without damage, to fight another day.

The traditional choices for dressing flies are natural fur and feather, but nowadays there is increasing use of man-made alternatives. Some might argue, 'If it ain't busted, don't mend it', but as will be seen in the course of this book, materials employed from the beginning of time to the present day tend to be chosen not so much for purposes of innovation as of practicality. Fly-tyers are opportunists: a new carpet may

look beautiful and suit the surrounding decor, but the colour could also be perfect for tying the body of a rough olive. A brace of pheasant may be a gourmet's delight, but the fly-tyer will be using the tail feathers long after the meal has faded from memory. An old electrical motor, of no further use to the mechanic, provides an endless source of ribbing and weighting for nymph patterns. No doubt similar scavenging tactics have been employed throughout history.

Fur and feather, the discarded by-products of human foodstuffs, were readily available and

sufficiently delicate in appearance to imitate the natural. Feather fibres wrapped around a hook and fished beneath the surface would move in the current, rather like the legs of the natural, while fur was ideal for constructing lifelike bodies. The feathers of most value to the fly-tyer come from around the bird's neck or back, called *hackle* and *saddle* respectively, the latter being larger and consequently better suited to tying the bigger wet flies, lures and streamers, the former reserved for more intricate patterns. Wet flies require the softness of hen feathers to impart that all-important movement under water; but that very softness is a disadvantage in a dry pattern, where the hackle and tail must support the weight of the hook upon the water's surface. Consequently, the dry patterns call for stiffer cock hackles of a very high quality – a rare commodity indeed.

The farmyard fowl of yesteryear were a far cry from the modern hybridised bird, being smaller, crossbred and thus offering greater

variety of coloration. A feather used in a successful dressing would be eagerly sought by other tyers, ceating a demand that breeders, both amateur and professional, would endeavour to satisfy. The humble farmyard mongrel must have been the source of feathers described in the old books. Indeed, as recently as 1933 the great G.E.M. Skues wrote: 'It is rather a tragedy that the general farmyard with its mixed breeds of fowls is gone . . . now there is nothing but whites and Rhode Island Reds.' Specialised breeding for egg and meat production had guaranteed its demise. Yet those same techniques that had so frustrated Skues were to prove of great benefit later, for by concentrating their skills on producing plumage rather than food, specialists can now provide an almost limitless supply of consistently perfect hackles.

So much for domestic poultry, but what of the more exotic feathers? With the advent of imperialism and colonialism, man travelled far and wide in his military and trading capacities. Army life and sporting instinct go hand in glove, so it is no surprise to find fly-fishers with a military background. Perhaps one of the first was Colonel Richard Venables, a Cromwellian soldier and contemporary of Isaak Walton. Three hundred years or so later Major Oliver Kite achieved fame as fisherman, author and broadcaster. Posted overseas, anglers used the materials indigenous to those countries as a source for tying their flies, bringing home examples of their work. Some of these feathers would horrify the modern conservationist – Indian jungle cock, the exotic ibis and marabou, now strictly preserved but formerly hunted for food and feather to the point of extinction – but at the time all were freely available, and it is unfair to judge with the benefit of hindsight. More common materials have been substituted for those of rare species, whilst captive breeding and regular harvesting of the feathers from those same birds supplies the balance.

Yet the variety of feathers is as nothing compared with the range of animal hair available. There are too many types to list, but, broadly speaking, virtually anything hairy will suffice for fly-tying; rat fur, admittedly, would appear

to be excluded, yet there are certainly a few that utilise the fur of polar bear. The reason that hair is so popular is that it offers such a wide choice of length, diameter, buoyancy and hue. And if the correct colour is not available, it lends itself to dyeing. Once again, anglers who imported patterns from another continent which called for native fur would simply substitute an acceptable common equivalent.

The growth of the petroleum industry, the invention of plastics and the consequent production of synthetic fibres, together with the expansion of retailing and mail-order facilities, have provided the fly-tyer with an ever-increasing range of materials, creating opportunities bounded only by his imagination. Perhaps the American dressers are most innovative in this respect; they have made elastic bug-legs, synthetic foam ant-bodies, and even perfectly formed polythene insect wings, complete with veining. The vegan fly-tyer can now dress artificial flies with a clear conscience, even if prohibited from using them. There is nothing really

new in the concept: just another example of the use of readily available material.

Fly-dressing is very much a hands-on craft and requires minimal equipment. The hook is held in a small clamp, called a vice, which allows the tyer to keep both hands free – one to hold the materials in place, the other to wind the thread (probably synthetic rather than traditional fine silk) around the hook in close turns as far as the bend, where any tail is offered up and secured with a couple more turns of thread to ensure a firm fixing. The other component parts of the pattern follow in sequence, working from the bend towards the eye, all necessary materials being tied in with a few turns of thread. Certain materials, such as the fine body-fur, will be *dubbed* or spun on to the thread, using a little wax and the natural twisting of the fibres for adhesion. This rope of fur and thread is then wound to form body or thorax. To protect the dressing, and also to impart a little glitter, metal or plastic tinsels are sometimes wound around the body. This is called *ribbing*.

When a pattern has to sink quickly to reach the fish feeding low in fast waters or at the bottom of a stillwater, an underlying bed of copper or lead is attached to the hook – either by winding (in the case of wire) or (with lead foil) by tying around with thread. After this part of the dressing is done, a head is formed behind the eye of the hook, the thread is tied off and then – and only then – the thread is cut. A coat of varnish applied to the head completes the dressing.

Most fly-fishermen with more than a passing interest tie their own flies at some stage of their angling career – indeed, many tie flies and never fish. Nor is it necessary to have the hands of a surgeon to enjoy the art. G.E.M. Skues, with fists like hams, would sit in the Fly-fishers' Club in London, tying perfect, diminutive patterns in his eighties. A vast majority of tyers are content to copy recognised patterns, but some achieve the supreme accolade – that of inventing a style of patterns so successful that it passes into common use. In this way the fisherman's armoury has evolved from the handful of flies mentioned in the *Treatysse* to the many hundreds in use today.

The art of fly-tying has incorporated many different fashions; from the Impressionism of the wet, through the Pre-Raphaelism of the dry and the Modernism of the nymph, to the Pop-Art of fluorescent lures. What follows is not intended to be an exhaustive catalogue of fly patterns – no such work can ever exist. Nor is it designed to be a recipe book – a number of such are already in print. It is a glimpse into the fascinating work of the fly-tyer's art.

RIVER TROUT

Dry Flies

Terrestrials

The *Hawthorn Fly* (above) is similar in size to a bluebottle, but is distinguished by its long trailing legs. It appears around the last week of April and continues through May, flourishing at the same time as the hawthorn blossom from which it gets its name. It is not a true aquatic insect, but attracts the attention of hungry early-season trout when blown on to the water. Cotton, who wrote the fly-fishing section in Isaak Walton's *The Compleat Angler*, mentions the 'thorn-tree fly', with black dubbed body mixed with 'eight or ten hairs of Isabella-coloured mohair' and mallard wings, which sounds rather similar. Unfortunately, he lists it as a fly for March, not April, but the description is closer than others mentioned in his April listings. In modern patterns the trailing legs are imitated by knotted feather fibres.

The humble ant sometimes appears on the water, particularly when swarms take to the wing, or where a river passes through woodland, in which case the fish may expect to see the occasional wood ant. Americans have very good imitative patterns but the British rely on a simpler approach, such as the *Ant* illustrated (centre) to represent the natural. It adequately simulates the general shape of the natural's head, thorax and abdomen, while the hackle supports the artificial and imitates the legs.

Although caterpillars form only a modest part of the trout's diet, they do occasionally fall from the foliage of bankside trees and will be devoured by fish sheltering beneath. Those found in Britain are predominantly green-yellow and consequently that is the principal colour in the artificials tied.

The *Caterpillar* pattern illustrated (below) uses yellow bucktail, tied in at the bend, doubled back along the hookshank and ribbed with green floss silk. The weight is as important as anything else on such a nondescript pattern, and this tying seems to make about the right disturbance when cast. An alternative pattern, certainly less fuss to tie, is simply a length of yellow chenille caught in just behind the eye of a bare hook and allowed to float freely. The mobility of the chenille imitates the movement of the natural as it struggles in its unfamiliar surroundings.

Daddy-Long-Legs

The daddy-long-legs, or, as it should properly be called, cranefly is another terrestrial which frequently loses the battle with the elements and finishes its life on the water surface, largely because it is a feeble flier. Cotton alludes to this fly in *The Compleat Angler*, using its old English name of Harry Long-Legs, and some authorities believe it to be the tenth fly mentioned in the *Treatysse*, although since the natural is easily caught and large enough to mount on a hook, it is more likely that our forebears fished the natural, a method still employed today. However, the sporting fly-fisher prefers to use the artificial Daddy, of which there is a wide choice, and which is satisfying to tie.

The patterns illustrated reflect the changes made by successive tyers. The *Natural Daddy* (above) has a raffia body wound directly on to the hookshank in open turns to simulate the segmented thorax of the natural. The wings are cree hackle points, a feather with alternating bars of red and black, and the whole is supported by a bushy hackle. The trailing legs of the natural are imitated with knotted fibres from a pheasant tail feather.

The *Fluorescent Red Dad's Daddy* (centre) has a detached hair-body, a method in which the hair is placed along a needle and bound with a thread. Once secured, the needle is removed from the centre and the finished body tied to the hookshank, allowing it to extend beyond the bend. As the naturals appear in greatest numbers in September, round about the trout's breeding season, the use of red is likely to appeal to the keen aggressive instincts of the fish.

The artificial legs are very delicate, breaking easily if caught by the trout's teeth, so most tyers add a couple of extras on the principle that trout cannot count. To overcome the problem, knotted monofilament, a far stronger alternative, may be substituted, as in the *Monofilament Daddy* (below) tied by Mr Wallis. Unfortunately, nothing is quite as realistic as the pheasant tail fibres, and anglers are normally content to suffer the damage caused by the teeth of the trout.

Grasshoppers

The grasshopper receives more attention from North American fly-fishers than from their British counterparts, but whereas the fashion for imitating the terrestrial insect is currently confined mainly to one side of the Atlantic, this has not always been the case. Charles Cotton mentions the *Grasshopper* (above) in *The Compleat Angler*. His pattern, simply tied with a green thread underbody palmered with a brown feather, obviously served him well, for it has survived the centuries and is popular in Ireland, where it is used as a dapping fly. Various British sources, including Courtney Williams, wax lyrical on the grasshopper for attracting the larger trout, and a grayling fly bearing the grasshopper name has been in use for some time. But to find realistic imitations, it is necessary to look at the American patterns.

The *Grasshopper* (centre) is an excellent example which utilises several different techniques. The head is deerhair, spun and clipped Muddler style, and dyed green at the front. The body is yellow wool, palmered with a brown feather trimmed close to simulate the legs. Knotted bunches of pheasant-tail fibres form the long hind legs, and the red flashed abdomen is suggested by a tag of red bucktail tied beneath a tag of body wool. The strip wing is of dark turkey feather.

The *Deerhopper* (below) is more impressionistic, relying on a body hackle to represent legs, spun yellow deerhair for the body, and a red-feather tail. The stiff wings, tied along either side, are strips of black turkey or crow.

Alder Fly

he *Alder Fly*, in both its dry and wet forms (above and below) has been in use, little changed, for more than 300 years, and is perhaps more important now than ever before, for the natural insect has proved to be less susceptible to pollution than other aquatic insects. Given its wide distribution and its appearance early on in the season, there is little wonder that this pattern is so popular. Many anglers confuse the natural with a sedge, and understandably so, for it has the sedge's tentlike wings and obviously tempts early-season trout wherever it is found. Although ostensibly a dry pattern, the artificial is commonly fished wet (or at least damp) as the natural only appears on water by accident, much in the same way as a terrestrial.

Blue-Winged Olive

Like the illustrious mayfly, the blue-winged olive is an upwinged fly but meets with less enthusiasm than its larger cousin. In fact, it is more important in many respects; its distribution is wider, it hatches earlier in the season, and hatches carry on long after the mayfly has disappeared. The natural is easily recognised by its brown-olive body, blue-grey wings and – a feature unique in an upwinged fly of its size – three tail filaments. Perhaps it is forgotten as soon as the mayfly appears, or maybe its notoriety for being a difficult insect to imitate has influenced thinking, but when the evening hatches occur – and they are as widespread as they are brief – the angler can ensure good sport. That it is a common fly may be judged by the many patterns devised through the ages.

Since G.E.M. Skues publicised the efficacy of the Orange Quill, it has been first choice for many fly-fishers wishing to imitate the female, particularly in the evening against a setting sun when the pattern seems to be at its best. However, the *Blue-Winged Olive Dun* (above) successfully imitates the principal features of both male and female. The wings are not solid feather slips, as in the traditional wet flies, for they would not suggest the translucency of the natural. Instead, the very tips of a blue-dun cock hackle are used which, combined with the red hackle and tail, create the correct impression.

Whereas both male and female are important to angler and trout alike when the dun is on the water, the male does not return to the water after mating (unless by accident) and may be dismissed as of no further importance, but the female receives the attention of both fish and tyer when she returns to lay her eggs. The *Sherry Spinner* (centre) is an excellent imitation, taking into account as it does the horizontal wings, overall colouring and, perhaps most importantly, the effect of the setting sun on the spent female.

So much for exact imitation, but hatches of the blue-winged olive last for a very short period, mainly in the evening, so the nymph, dun and spinner may well be on the water at the same time. As a result, many fly-fishers adopt a general pattern, and few dry flies are as tried and tested as a pattern from Devon, the *Pheasant Tail* (right). By chance, the three tails of the blue-winged olive are accurately represented in the Pheasant Tail, and both body shape and coloration are sufficient to pass all but the closest inspection of a fish which is likely to be feeding on both stages of the adult. As it is also used to simulate pale waterflies and small sedges, this is a general pattern in use throughout the UK.

Mayflies

The fly-fisher is more interested in the adult mayfly than the nymph. On the best waters, in good years, hatches of mayfly are so dense and the trout feed so heavily that the period is known as 'duffer's fortnight', for in such conditions it is virtually impossible to draw a blank. But when the main activity has diminished to a trickle, and the surviving fish have the time and temerity to inspect their food more closely, an exact imitation approach is called for. Principal features of the natural are the long, narrow segmented abdomen with three long setae, all of which is curved upward, and the tall wings held at an angle over the body. The female is bigger than the male and the dun is drab by comparison with the imago which has brilliant colouring and glossy wings.

The *Green Drake* (above) is tied to represent the male and the Yellow Drake the female of *E. dancia*. It owes its elegance to the curved duck breast feathers tied back to back and separated by a generous hackle. The body is olive floss which imparts both shine and smoothness, overwound with gold wire to simulate the segmentation of the thorax.

The *Lively Mayfly* (centre) uses a tying technique credited to an American, Chauncey Lively, and such patterns are alternatively named Detached Body Mayflies. Finest deerhair is mounted on a darning needle and ribbed with tying silk. The needle is then withdrawn and the completed section mounted on the hookshank, the pattern being finished in the normal way. Detached bodies have proved very successful and every year tyers seek new methods of construction. One of the latest techniques involves the use of latex glue, copydex, smeared on to a sheet of glass. When the latex has dried, it is carefully rolled to form a thin, pliable tube which may be coloured with marker pen before mounting on the hook to make the body.

The *Green Partridge Mayfly* (below) is a popular English style, one of many to utilise a hackle from the shoulder feathers of a French partridge. The body is palmered along its entire length with an olive feather.

Mayflies

The *Silhouette Mayfly* (above) has the appearance of the characteristic American Thorax patterns and relies on outline alone to suggest the natural. The wings are represented by a tuft of feather fibre tied upright and slightly divided, while the dubbed fur body falls halfway between the palmered and smooth-bodied styles. Probably it is a good dun imitation.

The spent female is imitated by another hackled pattern in the *French Partridge Spent Mayfly* (centre). The tail fibres of pheasant tail and deerhair are three times the length of the hook – not curved downward this time to drag in the water. The wings are hackle points, tied spent with a double hackling of light brown hen and French partridge feather. A cunning section of spun clipped deerhair, tied in at the end of the body, imitates the swollen egg sac of the natural and also ensures that the pattern does not become swamped.

The *Spent Black Drake* (below) is a simple yet eyecatching artificial – very much in the impressionistic class – which has a black feather fibre or hairwing tied at right angles to the hookshank by crossing the thread in a figure-of-eight pattern. A clipped, palmered body with contrasted ribbing and pheasant-tail setae completes the pattern. Incidentally, the alternative name for the mayfly – drake – is derived from the manner the body curves in much the same way as the wing of a male duck.

Olive Imitations

The large dark olive is an important early-season insect – important enough to be the first pattern on Halford's famous list and one with which Skues found little argument. The *Rough Olive* (above) is with us today, used in a variety of sizes throughout the season to represent any olive dun; and with its original tying of heron-herl body and cock hackle dyed olive, it would still be recognised by the old masters. As the heron is now a protected species, goose feather is the customary substitute.

The *Greenwell's Glory* (centre) is an excellent general pattern, tied and fished in both wet and dry styles. The original fly, designed by Canon William Greenwell in 1854, and tied by James Wright, a professional tyer on the famous River Tweed, was the wet pattern. It was representative of the dark olive dun and tied with split wings of blackbird, yellow silk body, and the Coch-y-bonddhu hackle (natural red with black centre and tips). By applying cobbler's wax to the silk, the yellow takes on the desired olive hue. Incidentally, it was common practice to use picric acid to dye fur and feather olive. Nowadays, life for the fly-tyer is somewhat easier; with a wide range of fabric dyes and a cosmetics industry preoccupied with changing the colour of women's hair, one is quite spoilt for choice. The *Dry Greenwell* (below) has a similar body, but the Coch-y-bonddhu hackle is replaced by a twin winding of furnace and medium-blue dun.

Sedge Imitations

Once deer hair has been spun on to the hookshank, it may be trimmed to almost any shape. Goddard and Henry studied the silhouette of the sedgefly which skitters invitingly across the water's surface at the end of the day, and sculpted their G & H Sedge (above) from a deerhair base, adding an underbody of green seal's fur and whisks of grey-brown hackle fibres, the uncut ends of which form the antennae. The end result is a virtually unsinkable fly which creates a lifelike wake when retrieved.

The G & H Sedge represents a radical departure from the accepted sedge imitations and in many respects is similar to the Muddler Minnow, another deerhair pattern where shape is used to create an illusion.

The *Elk Hair Sedge* (centre), from the Orvis Company, combines an old technique, palmering, with buoyant elk hair to present an impression of the natural. The hair, flaring over the body in a delta shape to emulate the wings, combines a good silhouette with excellent floatability.

Although the sedge is not the best of fliers and does create a disturbance on the water in its attempts to become airborne, no fish would expect a natural to land with the gusto of a heavily dressed artificial, particularly on quiet waters where a gentler approach is called for. Consequently, a parachute hackle was a logical addition to the series. The *Parachute Sedge* (below) will land lightly, present a good impression of the natural, and float all day.

Sedges

The sedge, or caddisfly, like the mayflies, attracts imitation at all stages of its life cycle. Because the species of the natural are legion (188 in Britain alone), history tends to favour the general approach: the 'Dun Cut' of the *Treatysse* would come under this heading. By the time Skues mentioned his reluctance to imitate the pupal stage (which seems strange for a nymphing man), imitations had doubtless been around for centuries in one form or another.

The *Wickham's Fancy* is a pattern apt to create confusion and some mystery. Many regard it as a fancy pattern – certainly it has the look and vintage of such flies – but it should properly be regarded as a general imitative pattern as it has gained a good reputation in both dry and wet forms (above and centre). Its origin is claimed by Dr T.C. Wickham, who instructed Winchester fly-tyer Hammond to tie examples which he fished on the River Test in Hampshire. Unfortunately, another Winchester tyer, George Correll, announced that he was tying the same pattern in 1884 for one Captain John Wickham. So the mystery remains.

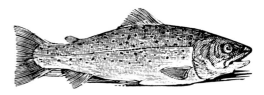

On its day, the Dry Wickham is a useful fly, probably attributable to its palmered body and split wings of starling feathers which afford the fly a tempting profile. Devotees will use the dry version when fish are preoccupied with small insects on the surface, an unhappy situation for the angler, known as smutting. Oddly enough, a complete contrast in size frequently works in such circumstances, and the Wickham's is just that. The wet version was popular on stillwaters to imitate sedge pupae, though with the development of nymph fishing in the twentieth century its popularity waned.

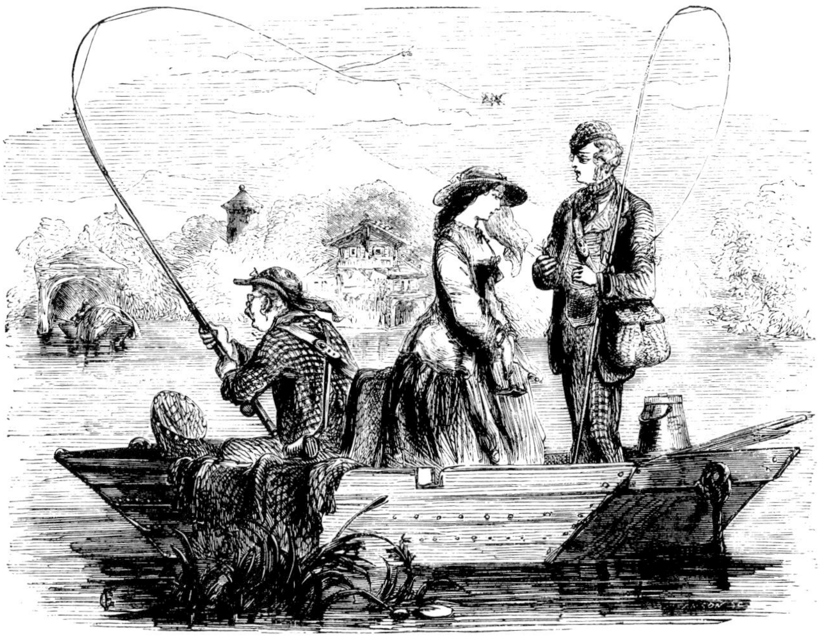

Fly-Tying Equipment

Fly-tying requires little equipment and minimal space. Properly organised devotees will acquire a desk or bench, the centrepiece of which is the tying vice; this is obtainable in various forms and qualities but is essentially a sprung-collet type of clamp on a long stem. It holds the hook securely and masks the point, leaving the hands free to hold the materials and tying thread. More sophisticated versions have quick-release levers and interchangeable jaws to accommodate all hook sizes from the largest salmon irons to the tiniest midge hooks.

The bobbin holder is a thin, smooth tube through which passes the thread. The spool is held in position by a pair of sprung arms. A brass weight provides a convenient point for grasping the holder and ensures that the thread stays under tension when the holder is released.

This basic ensemble is completed by a pair of fine, sharp scissors (two pairs, in fact, are preferable, one for cutting delicate hackles, the other for quill, tinsels and wire) and a dubbing needle – essentially a darning needle mounted on a handle for picking out the dubbing, separating feather fibres, applying varnish and a host of other jobs.

Additional gadgets may include sprung tweezers or hackle pliers to hold the tip of a feather while winding the hackle, and a hair stacker – two small, smooth tubes – to ensure the tips of hair are correctly aligned after cutting. Both jobs may equally well, or better, be done with the fingers. Finally, a good anglepoise lamp will illuminate the work in hand, and a magnifying glass on a snake neck may be helpful when tying smaller patterns.

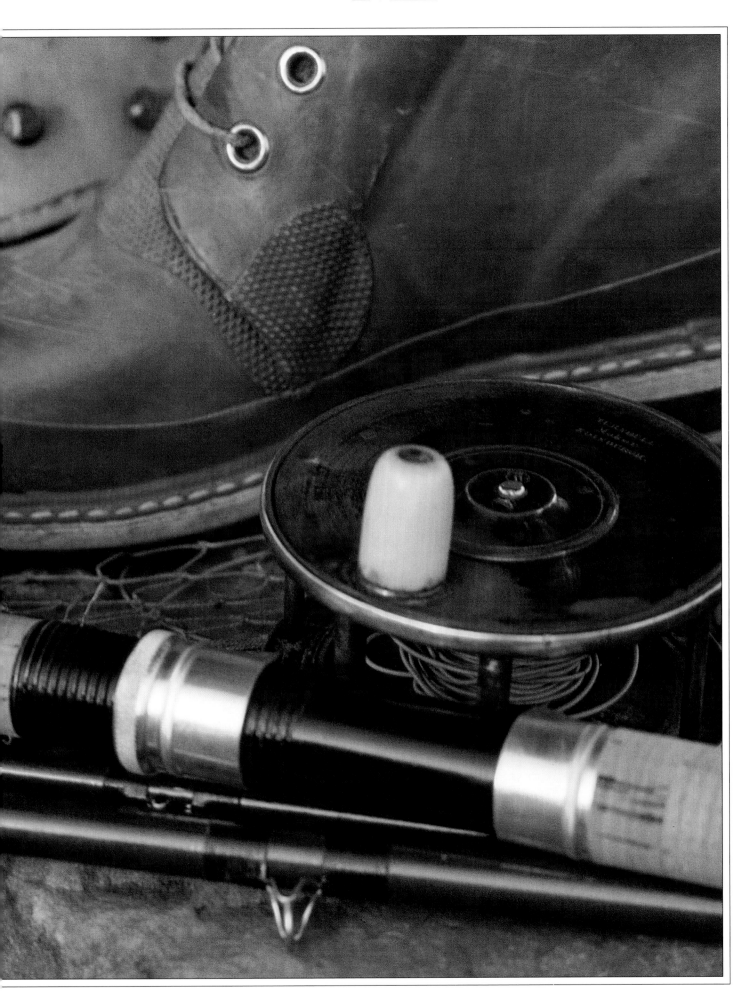

Coch-Y-Bonddhu

The *Coch-y-bonddhu*, pronounced *cothee-bondoo* (above) is a centuries-old Welsh pattern representing a beetle, although it is not clear which species is intended. An English translation of the Welsh, 'red with black trunk', does not help any more than a search for a beetle of that name, since it is used to describe different species in different regions. The Welsh name is a particularly apt description of the hackle feather used in its tying, which has a black centre and red outer tipped with black. The name is now used for both pattern and feather. The eminent angler-entomologist John Goddard identifies the beetle as *Phylloperta horticula*, a species indigenous to Wales and Scotland, also known as the June bug or bracken clock. In any case, none of this really matters, as the pattern used by fly-fishers is a general one designed to imitate any beetles unfortunate enough to land on a trout's dining table.

The *Grey Duster* (below) is a popular general dry fly, particularly on streams and fast rivers. Various authorities suggest that fish take this deceiver for insects ranging from mayfly to midge, so the secret probably lies in the sizes used. The body is always blue rabbit fur and the hackle is badger cock, the only variant appearing to be a parachute version.

Halford's Gnat

Halford's *Black Gnat* (above) is still a good copy of the small black fly *Bibio johannis*, although trout will happily assume it to represent any black fly of similar appearance.

Halford suggested the use of latex bodies but was disappointed with the material available at the time. Modern dressers have discovered dental latex, a thin rubber sheeting which does not degrade when wet and readily accepts colour from a fibre-tip pen. Accordingly, its use has proliferated, particularly in the nymph patterns such as the *Latex Grub* (below). The latex comes in coloured sheets but a tinted floss underbody or the use of coloured marking pens is probably more efficient. A dubbed thorax of hare's fur adequately represents the sedge or caddis which live within a protective case built from silt, gravel, twigs or anything that comes readily to hand. Tied on large hooks, similar patterns are effective on stillwater.

Such small patterns present the tyer with the greatest difficulties. Small hooks of these dimensions cannot be accommodated by the ordinary vice, and a smaller clamp is inserted into the jaws. Normal thread is too bulky – only the finest of silks are used but these are the most easily broken. Nor are such patterns easy to fish with, for the thickness of the monofilament leader, and therefore its strength, must be proportional to the size of hook used. Two pounds of fighting-fit trout on the end of a one-pound breaking strain leader is quite a challenge.

Skues Patterns

G. E.M. Skues fished for trout on the Itchen while a scholar at Winchester College in 1875, but it was not until he qualified as a solicitor, when a client offered him fishing on the famous Abbot's Barton stretch of the river in 1883, that he was able to devote himself to his favourite chalkstream. These were the years when the influence of Halford's dry-fly theories were at their height, theories which were hardened by his followers into rigid dogma, treating any subsurface angling with disdain. In his *Fly Fishing in Theory and Practice,* Halford had doubted the efficacy of using the artificial nymph, arguing that it was too difficult to construct patterns which accurately imitated the movement of the natural.

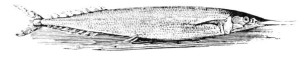

Using the same techniques of observation and study advocated by the Master, Skues picked up the gauntlet, successfully tying and fishing nymphs and employing his prodigious writing skills to publicise his techniques. This audacity provoked such ire in the purists that his crusade for a more liberal attitude to fly-fishing eventually led to his being driven from his beloved Itchen at the age of eighty. Nevertheless, before he died in 1949, aged ninety-one, he was recognised as one of the world's greatest exponents of fly-fishing. Apart from a mountain of books, articles and correspondence on all aspects of the sport, Skues's legacy includes important patterns, both dry-fly and nymph, still used today.

The blue-winged olive is a common enough fly but notoriously difficult to imitate. Whereas Skues never actually claimed to have invented the *Orange Quill* (above), it was he who discovered and publicised its effectiveness when the duns are hatching. His version of his fly, of which he was justifiably proud to his dying day, is today still very much in use.

The *Little Red Sedge* (below) has a marvellously antique look, imparted by the palmered hackle.

Dulverton and Blagdon

The Beige, which originated in 1917, was tied in the Exmoor village of Dulverton by a member of the Wills family home on leave from the Somme. Peter Deane altered the original and renamed it the *Beacon Beige* (above) after Culmstock Beacon, which overlooked his home. But things change slowly in the west country, and you can still visit Dulverton and buy the original tying. Deane's version, however, is widely regarded as an excellent imitation of the olive dun.

A little farther east, nestled in the Mendips, is Blagdon, scene of an important revolution in game fishing. Growing cities required water, and Blagdon Lake was formed at the turn of the century to supply nearby Bristol. Stocked with trout, these reservoirs were to give ordinary folk an opportunity to enjoy what had increasingly become an elitist sport. When Blagdon opened in 1904, anglers relied on the techniques of river and loch fishing, using winged wet flies, but specialised methods gradually evolved together with a new breed of angler – the stillwater fisherman.

Dr H.A. Bell is to the stillwater man what Skues is to the river angler. A general practitioner in Wrington and Blagdon, Bell started fishing Blagdon Lake in 1922, continuing until the 1960s. Every Friday and Sunday, and stopping only for a packed lunch, he studied the insect life and its occurrence in the trout's stomach. Utilising these observations, he created his famous *Amber Nymph* (centre) to imitate the population of sedge pupae and, recognising the importance of the midge pupa in stillwaters (perhaps the first to do so), introduced the Blagdon Buzzer, upon which all the alternative patterns are based. Obviously, Dr Bell refused to be limited by the restraints of exact imitation, and his *Grenadier* (below), a general nymphing pattern, testifies to the fact. It is a great pity that he never committed his knowledge to print, but his importance is remembered by fly-fishermen who visit Blagdon whenever they see Dr Bell's bush on the southern bank. Presumably his patients were careful not to fall sick on those days he fished.

William Lunn

It is not surprising that, in addition to professionals and amateur enthusiasts, river-keepers have an interest in fly-tying. William Lunn was responsible for the Houghton stretch of the River Test, the famous Hampshire chalkstream. Although he started tying flies rather late in life, Lunn has left us with quite a few patterns still in use today, the most famous – or easily remembered – of which is *Lunn's Particular* (above). Created in 1917, it has all the features of the classic dry: the slim body of Rhode Island Red hackle stalk, a long tail and neat hackle from the same source, and blue-dun hackle tips tied spent to imitate the medium olive and large dark olive spinners.

His *Houghton Ruby* (centre) imitates the female iron-blue spinner and again he uses a hackle stem (in this instance dyed crimson) to represent the segmented body of the natural.

An important fly on southern waters is a large sedge called the caperer, which puts in an appearance during the evening in the latter part of the season. Lunn created an artificial of the same name, *Caperer* (below), and gave it the alternative tag of Welshman's Button. This is a misnomer, for the latter is a different sedge fly altogether – much smaller and darker than the caperer, and appearing a month or two earlier than its big cousin. Moreover, neither of the naturals has a band of yellow around the thorax. So why the artificial? Perhaps Lunn decided to part with tradition and create an impressionistic sedge pattern. Whatever his motives, the Caperer is very successful on both river and stillwater the length and breadth of the country.

Adams and Irresistibles

The *Adams* (above) emerged in 1922, tied by Leonard Halladay of Michigan for C.E. Adams, to imitate the flying ant. By the time Ray Bergman published his famous work *Trout* in 1932, numerous versions had appeared which, tied in a range of sizes, represented anything from sedges to midges, and it found favour among European anglers. The upright wings are simulated by the points of a grizzle hackle, whilst the spun body, in the style of the Hendrickson, is of natural grey muskrat.

The Irresistible series is attributed to either of two Americans, Joe Messenger or Kenneth Lockwood. Popularised in the 1950s, it is not dissimilar to the Rat-Faced MacDougal, but its origins lie in the Wulff pattern; substituting a wool body for clipped deerhair offers a similar silhouette but with greater buoyancy. The wings may be a simple tuft of hair or hackle points tied upright or spent. Changes in wing and hackle coloration give the pattern its various names and, as with so many other patterns, the Irresistibles are used for trout fishing in their smaller sizes and for salmon when tied on larger-sized hooks. The *White Irresistible* (centre), with its buoyancy and highly visible white tuft, is ideal for imitating sedges in fast, broken water.

Replacing the tuft of white hair with the more conventional wings of feather makes it possible to combine the body of the Irresistibles with proven patterns such as the Adams, thus creating the *Adams Irresistible* (below).

Flyboxes

Once the flies have been tied, a further storage system must be employed to ensure the finished articles reach the water's edge in pristine condition. In former days, when casts were made of gut, the angler would carry both flies (albeit usually wet patterns) and casts in dampened envelopes to retain their pliability. Cast carriers are still used, particularly when fishing wet-flies in a team of three, but as water retention is no longer a criterion, the leader is simply wound on to anything from a simple beer mat to a preformed plastic holder. But with the plethora of patterns and hook sizes nowadays available, the angler may well have hundreds of flies which are best stored in a library case, to be called on as required. This is made of wood and lined with ethafoam or spring clips, and may be tiered for extra accommodation. For the itinerant river-fisher, wandering the bank with a minimum of equipment, various pocket-sized cases are available, made either of wood (aesthetically pleasing but heavy), aluminium (lightweight but prone to condensation which corrodes the hook) or plastic (light, buoyant and inexpensive but also subject to condensation, and hardly uplifting to the spirits). The aluminium box, made universally popular by Peter Wheatley, is probably the best and comes in a wide variety of styles to satisfy most anglers. There is, for example, the dual-purpose type favoured by the trout fisher; ethafoam lined lid for wet flies and nymphs, and compartments with clear lids, spring-hinged, to accommodate dry flies without damaging the hackles. Provided damp flies are dried, either in hatband or sheepskin patch, before being returned to the box, this is an ideal accessory.

R. S. Austin

Two of the patterns devised by the celebrated Devonshire fly-tyer, R.S. Austin, publicised by Skues, are still in use today, albeit with slight variations. His *Blue Upright* (above) tied on the larger sizes is an excellent imitation of the large dark olives, whilst the smaller sizes are popular representations of the iron blue dun.

Apparently, the Half Stone was originally tied as a wet fly to copy the sedge pupa, but fished dry it is a fair representation of the smaller stoneflies, the species which are of more importance to the angler fishing the stony upland rivers found in Austin's part of the country than they are to the chalkstream man. The contradiction is more apparent than real: fished on a tumbling stream, this style soon becomes damp, if not actually wet, so that it is probably better classified as a general pattern. In fact, it bears some resemblance to Austin's more famous Tup's Indispensable: the rear two-thirds of the body is yellow floss silk, the front mole's fur picked out with blue-dun hackle and tails. It is certainly from Austin's bench and has been catching trout for a century. The version illustrated, the *Honey Half Stone* (below), is tied with lighter tail and hackle.

The Angler's Curse

The diminutive insects which make up the *Caenis* family usually make an appearance on rivers in the morning and on lakes in the late afternoon. They are truly the bane of the fly-fisher. Their minute size is inversely proportional to the vast numbers hatching and the consequent interest shown by feeding trout, and accordingly they have been named the Angler's Curse. A sensible fisherman would pack up and head for home as soon as these insects appear at the end of a day's fishing, but to the philosophical angler they present something of a challenge. The aptly named *Last Hope* (above) and its duskier brother, the *Dark Last Hope* (below), are dressings introduced by one such intrepid angler, John Goddard; they are fished wet to represent the emerger and dry for the dun.

Vincent Marinaro

In 1950, Vincent Marinaro published *A Modern Dry-Fly Code*. Marinaro fished limestone rivers, the American equivalent of the English chalkstreams, and after studying the prevailing fly styles he questioned the wisdom of heavy hackling to represent legs, bunches of fibres for the tails, and patterns tied on large hooks. He argued that a heavy hackle used to simulate the insect's legs masked the outline of the wings and the true body colouring. The British style of sparse tails was preferable to represent the setae of the original, none of which, he contended, were bigger than a size 14 hook. Continuing, he made the point that increased pollution had diminished the population of aquatic insects available to fish, which were turning instead to terrestrials for the bulk of their diet. So Marinaro's *Code* criticised both old and comparatively new practices in flytying, suggesting instead a radical departure in style and size.

Most of his ideas are to be found in the modern Thorax flies, in which the wings are tied midway between the eye and the bend of the hook, and two strands of feather fibres form the widely spaced setae.

Many of the traditional dry flies have benefited from Marinaro's style of dressing, regardless of their vintage. In chronological order, the patterns illustrated are the *March Brown* (above), *Blue-Winged Olive* (centre) and the *Adams* (below). Tyers will often test their dry fly patterns by dropping them on to a flat surface to see if they land correctly. Some are better than others but the Marinaro Thorax patterns rarely, if ever, fail the acid test.

Spinners

Swisher & Richards's *Selective Trout*, published in 1971, developed Marinaro's argument of pattern profile, suggesting that the hackle masked the wing and body outline, key trigger points to a fish. Their *no-hackle dun* utilised Marinaro's idea of a split tail, well separated to impart balance, a polypropylene dubbed body and split wings, again flared for balance. These basic concepts are to be found in a series of general Spinner patterns which, if tied in a range of colours and sizes, may adequately represent most of the naturals.

The patterns illustrated, *Olive Spinner* (above), *Cream Spinner* (centre) and *Black Spinner* (below), are tied with feather fibres for the tail and wings, although artificial substitutes are perfectly suitable: indeed, polypropylene fibres have a lower specific gravity than water and, unlike feathers, are not absorbent. The material, known variously as poly-yarn or poly-wing, is easily available, as are good alternatives for the tail fibres – microfibbets – finely tapered nylon fibres of the type used for paintbrushes, and in a variety of hues. The plastics industry also supplies the dubbing for the body.

All these patterns have the same style of tying. The tail fibres are tied in, and dubbing is applied to the thread and wound along to the wing position where those fibres are secured and separated by passing the dubbed thread in a figure-of-eight design which also builds up the thorax. The dubbing finishes just before the eye of the hook and is tied off in the usual way.

The range of colours available ensures that most of the spinners may be imitated, and these patterns are especially useful in smaller sizes to imitate the diminutive naturals which are so difficult to identify.

Wulff Patterns

The *Grey Wulff* (above) is not so much a specific imitation as a style of dressing. Here we see a unique approach from America, first fished in 1930 and still going strong worldwide sixty years later. Lee Wulff reacted against the patterns of the time, believing they offered little in the way of meat to a hungry fish. He augmented the body size, used bucktail – a material far more durable and buoyant than feather – for wings and tail, and increased the hackle size to support the extra weight. The result was a true classic.

Because the pattern is generic rather than specific, fly-tyers are not confined slavishly to following a published recipe. Varying the materials, colour and dimensions creates endless possibilities. To mention just a few, the body may be constructed of fur (mole, rabbit, musk-rat and mink are common), wool, peacock herl, floss or synthetic substitutes. On stillwaters in a flat calm, tied small with brown squirrel tail to replace the bucktail, the Wulff will tempt a cautious trout. On fast-flowing moorland streams it rides high and dry, whilst tied large it is an effective mayfly pattern. It is also used as a salmon fly in both wet and dry forms. Standard patterns, if there can be such things, include the *White Wulff* (centre) tied with white hair and fur, and the *Red Wulff* (below).

Wulff Patterns

Other tested variants of the Wulff pattern include the *Grizzly Wulff* (above), utilising the ever-popular yellow floss body with grizzle hackle, and the *Royal Wulff* (centre), an attractor tied with a body of peacock herl banded with red floss.

Lee Wulff insists that in all examples of the series the wings should be tied upright, not slanting forward. The exception to this rule, however, is the *Grey Wulff Mayfly* (below), in which the winging imitates that all-important characteristic of the natural.

Surely no other series has achieved such recognition – a pattern which is popular with trout and salmon fishers alike – on both sides of the Atlantic.

Oliver Kite

After leaving the army, Major Oliver Kite pursued a fishing career, gaining wide popularity during the 1960s as a broadcaster (he appeared in his own series on British television) and writer. As successful on stillwater as river, Kite continued the nymphing traditions of Skues and Sawyer, but his no-nonsense approach to fishing is best illustrated by the fact that he is remembered for just two patterns, one a dry, the other a nymph. *Kite's Imperial* (above), devised in 1962, may well represent the dark olive dun but it is really a general pattern, favoured by Kite in all conditions, and a strong contender for those who fish all season, using one pattern exclusively. The original dressing required heron herl for the body, a thorax ribbed with gold wire, and a tail and hackle of honey-dun cock, but the heron is nowadays protected and grey goose feather used as a substitute.

Kite's *Bare Hook Nymph* (below) is the very antithesis of everything the great Halford stood for: it is simply a bare hook with a thorax of copper wire. Nevertheless, the major would use it to demonstrate Sawyer's *induced take* technique. The idea is to cast upstream, allowing the nymph to drift down to a position just in front of the fish. At that precise moment the rod is lifted, causing the nymph to rise towards the surface, and that is enough to induce the fish to take. Easier said than done? Not for Major Kite – he demonstrated with a paper bag covering his head!

Gold-Ribbed Hare's Ear

The *Gold-Ribbed Hare's Ear* (above in nymphal form, and centre), attributed to the Victorian tyer James Ogden, is one of the few patterns to be universally adopted by dry and wet enthusiasts alike. The origins are lost, but it has certainly been around for a couple of centuries. Traditionally, the patterns use fur from the rabbit's ear, mingling the longer guard hairs with the lighter-coloured underfur and dubbing for a body, to give the imitation a very buglike appearance. Fished below the surface, the Gold-Ribbed Hare's Ear is a general nymphing pattern. Fished in the surface film, it may be taken for a hatching sedge, whilst fished dry (or rather, damp) it is a good olive imitation. The fur body is picked out with a needle, enabling the guard hairs to mimic legs, and whereas various sources make mention of a hackled version, it is generally tied without. The great F.M. Halford dallied for a while before dismissing it because it did not represent a specific insect. This pattern is so easy to tie, and so widely imitated, that it would appear to be impossible to alter in any way. Not so, for the American version, the *Gold-Ribbed Hare's Ear Nymph* (below), which favours a long-shanked hook, retains the hare's ear in name alone, using instead rabbit's underbody fur.

Storage

As the tyer's stock of materials grows, the matter of storage becomes pressing. A plastic envelope with a zip fastening, available in a variety of sizes, is very practical for keeping materials flat and pest-free. These may then be stored in a card-file index system or in biscuit tins – depending on the degree of sophistication required – but preferably in logical and easily accessible order. The smallest materials, such as tippet feathers, bug legs, ethafoam balls and even hooks can be put in the same envelopes, attached to a card and stored in a roladex-type filing system. The materials are thereby protected from dust, dirt, physical damage and vermin, whilst being readily retrievable; the aesthetic level varies from the Heath Robinson to elegant custom-built tying desks.

Most fly-fishers seem to suffer from a peculiar paranoia: no matter how well researched the water, no matter how judicious the fly selection, on the day the vital pattern will be at home, languishing in the stock-box. One tested antidote to this disorder is to travel with a portable fly-tying kit which contains a vice and other vital accessories, together with the most commonly used threads, tinsels, furs and feathers. Various sizes are obtainable, choice being dictated by the duration and nature of the fishing trip. The patient can then fish happily all day, knowing that tomorrow's success may be enhanced by a fly-tying session that evening.

An alternative remedy is a wallet-sized kit containing miniaturised equipment and a sample of materials for bankside use. Experts would probably spurn the vice in such situations and resort to finger and thumb to hold the hook.

Iron Blue

J immie Wright must have been a devout man as well as an excellent fly-tyer, for another of his patterns, this time a celebrated salmon fly, used hair from a dog owned by a minister. The dog was called Gary, hence the fly's name, *Gary Dog* (above), but it is known variously as Minister's Golden or Yellow Dog. It is tempting to wonder whether the cleric in question could have been Canon Greenwell at the beginning of his career.

The iron blue, or *Baetis niger* and *Baetis muticus*, which are the scientific denominations of the two insects that share the common name, has been important to fly-fishers in Britain for at least 400 years. Accordingly, there are myriad patterns of *Iron Blue Dun* (centre) available to the tyer, typified by the pattern illustrated. However, it is worth considering some of the materials utilised in the past: bodies of stripped condor, heron or peacock herl, mole or rat fur; wings of starling, cormorant, water hen, tomtit's tail or swift's quill feather – the list is quite remarkable. The dry-fly fisher would use the *Dry Iron Blue* (below), easily recognised by its red rump, to tempt his quarry.

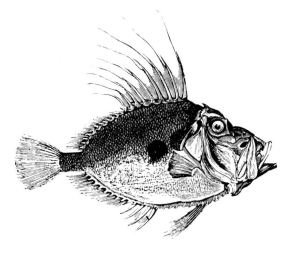

RIVER TROUT

Wet Flies

March Brown

The *March Brown* (above) is one of the earliest naturals to appear, both on the water and in the annals of angling literature. The *Treatysse of Fysshynge* recommends the 'Dun Fly' under the entry for March, Cotton (likewise grouping his patterns under monthly headings) makes mention of it, and it has been with us ever since. The natural is confined to the fast, rocky streams of upland districts and this, coupled with its appearance so early in the season, tends to persuade authorities to dismiss the artificial's value as an imitative pattern, suggesting instead that it more resembles various sedges. The influence of the dry fly disciples, which predominated in late Victorian and Edwardian circles, was very strong, and it is easy for us, therefore, to gain the impression that the use of imitative dry flies was the sole province of the southern lowland angler. This is not the case, however, for to the angler who early in the season fishes a stream or river where the March Brown is indigenous, its appearance is as important as that of the mayfly on the chalkstreams. When hardier souls imitate a hatch of the natural with the *Dry March Brown* (centre), the chalkstream man has another month to wait before his season opens. The *March Brown Nymph* is illustrated below.

Partridge and Snipe

The Partridge series comprises the Orange, Yellow, Blue, Black, Claret and Green, of which the *Partridge and Orange* (above) is the most popular, both on fast streams and stillwaters. Although the series has been around a long time, the Orange is a comparatively new dressing of the old February Red, the Dun Fly mentioned in the *Treatysse*, but its supporters would argue that it is suggestive of various aquatic creatures, from stoneflies to shrimps. The Partridge and Yellow requires a slightly lighter shade of feather but retains the same gold wire ribbing. This fly, along with the Partridge and Blue, probably represent something similar to their equivalents in the Snipe series, although John Roberts, an authority on fishing ephemera, suggests that the Blue is extremely successful. Others in this series, as in so many others, enjoy considerably less popularity.

Along with the Partridge and Orange, the *Snipe and Purple* (centre) is perhaps the most popular fly of its type for trout and grayling fishing on the river. The choice of hackle feather (examples below) is reputedly most important – correct tying calls for a dark feather from the covert, or wing's edge – but a well-tied specimen is supposed to represent the iron blue dun. Its fairer brother, the Snipe and Yellow, tied with a body of yellow floss silk, can be useful to imitate the paler duns.

Palmers

Aptly named, the *Zulu* (above) is a fearsome-looking thing. Its palmered body and red tag are reminiscent of the medieval flies of the *Treatysse* and Cotton. In loch-style fishing, where a team of three flies is trailed on a long leader, the pattern fished closest to the surface is called the *bob fly*, probably because it bobs on the surface. *Palmering*, one of the earliest styles of dressing mentioned in print from the *Treatysse* onwards, is the winding of a hackle feather in open turns around the body of the artificial to give a bushy appearance. It is a particularly effective technique when imitating the sedges which make quite a commotion on the surface while attempting to fly. Palmered flies such as the Zulu lend themselves well to being fished in the bob position.

Exactly when the Zulu came into being is a mystery; it has the look of a fly which Cotton may have used, but the name, presumably derived from its colouring and current events, implies that it was christened, if not devised, during the Zulu Wars of the late nineteenth century. That it is not popular in Scotland and Ireland provides some idea of its origins – the older patterns did not benefit from the enhanced communication of the contemporary media and, rather like the populace, tended towards the parochial. The popularity evoked by the Zulu is reflected by the variations: the gold version is no longer utilised but the *Blue Zulu* (centre) is in current use.

The *Soldier Palmer* (below) is arguably the most widely used palmered artificial and has been a successful bob fly for generations of stillwater anglers. The traditional red wool is increasingly replaced by fluorescent material to increase visibility but otherwise the Soldier Palmer remains unchanged. The pattern is at least 150 years old, some authors suggesting that its name reflects the uniform worn by contemporary British soldiers, the Redcoats.

Bumbles

The palmered patterns known as Bumbles are old, if not ancient. They originate in Derbyshire and were mentioned by Charles Cotton, companion of Isaak Walton. Surviving the centuries, they were adopted by Halford who turned them into dry patterns before they came to the attention of an Irish fisherman, T.C. Kingsmill-Moore. The latter combined the overall style with a subtlety of colouring – the hallmark of the best Irish flies – by using multiple hackles and coloured seal's fur to create soft, translucent, general patterns which the lough trout found so inviting.

His masterpiece is the *Golden Olive Bumble* (above) which combines gold-olive and red palmering with dyed guinea fowl throat hackles over an olive seal's fur body and a tail of golden pheasant topping. The *Claret Bumble* (centre) is similarly tied, but the body is claret and the palmering a combination of claret and black.

The *Silver and Blue* (below) is more akin to the original Derbyshire patterns, and although the silver body is lightly palmered with a light blue hackle, this version has the sleek look of a northern wet fly, which is precisely what it is. The Bumbles have a good reputation for trout fishing but the Silver and Blue is popular with grayling anglers.

Butchers

The Butcher series has an interesting history. It was originally called Moon's Fly when it was created by Messrs Jewhurst and Moon, but the name was changed in 1838 to reflect Mr Moon's trade in Tunbridge Wells, Kent. In the standard *Butcher* (above) the red tag is reputed to represent meat, while the blue is the colour of a butcher's apron, but as it was tied to imitate fry, that seems a rather romantic notion. The original dressing used fibres from a kingfisher's wing, a throwback to the days when that beautiful bird was considered to be a pest on fishing waters, to create the *Kingfisher Butcher* (centre), but modern dressings use a jay's wing or a feather dyed blue. To ring the changes, the blue whisks are replaced with red, creating the *Bloody Butcher* (below), whereas changing the body from silver to gold creates the Gold Butcher.

Without doubt, the Butchers are effective patterns (as attested by their survival for the better part of two centuries) on both stillwater and river. The grey wings which are such a feature of this series are taken from a drake's wing, although the tail, originally of red ibis, is now a harmless dyed substitute. Apart from the wings, the Butchers share a reputation for being at their best at the start and finish of the season, suggesting that they are taken as fry imitations.

Red patterns are most effective late in the season; on stillwaters they attract fish feeding avidly on fry, whilst river trout seem to attack a red imitation out of aggression. As a fry imitation, it is worthwhile comparing the Butcher to the more modern imitative patterns; it may look crude beside its younger counterparts, but the question must be asked – will the others survive two centuries hence?

Scottish Loch Flies

The *Blae and Black* (above) is another pattern used both for trout and sea trout, presenting those fish with an insect-like morsel. Its history is vague, some attributing its origin to Ireland, but the use of the word *blae* to describe the bluish hue of the wing, and the fact that an early-season midge of the same name appears in Scotland, would seem to indicate a Scottish heritage. As with other similar patterns, the ribbing can be altered to create the Blae and Silver and the Blae and Gold.

The *Dunkeld* (centre) is a pattern which has made the transition from salmon fly to trout fly – not a particularly rare occurrence when dealing with the attractor styles. The beautifully marked winging is the cheek-feather of the jungle cock. Various substitutes are available, including one which involves painting the 'eye' on to a suitable feather with enamel paint.

Originally called The Lady of the Lake, the *Alexandra* (below) underwent a change of name in honour of Queen Alexandra. It is an old fancy pattern which has certainly been around since the 1850s, and although the bright colours seem calculated to catch the eye of the angler in a tackle shop as much as that of a fish, it enjoyed quite a reputation in its day. It is tied in a range of sizes to attract both trout and salmon, and though probably not as popular now, it is regularly used as a stillwater lure to imitate fry.

Scottish Loch Flies

James Ogden, of Gold-Ribbed Hare's Ear fame, tied the famous *Invicta* pattern (above), quite deadly as a hatching sedge, and he was the first man to introduce (in print, anyway) the split-wing technique utilised today. The use of two matching strips – called *slips* – of feather would replace the folded single strip previously employed and would cause future generations of fly-tying novices immeasurable heartache and frustration. The same man purports to be the first to tie a dry fly, stating in his 1879 publication *Ogden on Fly-tying* that he had been using floating flies since 1839.

The *Peter Ross* (centre), named after its Scottish originator, is a version of the Teal and Red and imitates the fry on which larger fish prey. Its popularity as a loch fly is shared by sea trout anglers in England, who consider it to be an essential pattern in their flybox.

The *Mallard and Claret* (below) is a pattern which has become the basis for a series. It was probably created by William Murdoch, an Aberdeenshire angler, and obviously does not represent any particular food form – which may account for its success on loch, lake and river for both trout and sea trout. The fly takes its name from the winging material – mallard – and the colour of the body – originally of seal's fur. By changing the body colour, the alternative, though less worthy, Mallard and Yellow, Mallard and Red, Mallard and Silver and Mallard and Green are created.

Favourites and Fancies

acklists are obviously keen fishermen and are ideally positioned to publicise any patterns they happen to create. Messrs Hardy introduced the *Hardy's Favourite* (above), a fancy pattern devised by J.J. Hardy for trout and sea trout fishing. It is interesting in that it dispenses with a conventional hackle in favour of a dark partridge, although the body is similar to the Royal Coachman. None of the old fancy patterns would look complete without the almost prerequisite tail of golden pheasant tippet feathers.

The same company added to the Butcher series, creating *Hardy's Gold Butcher*, still in use today as a point fly on stillwaters, reputedly working when others in the series have failed.

The *Watson's Fancy* (below) is a traditional Scottish wet fly used on the lochs to catch both trout and the migrating sea trout. At a glance, it appears to be similar to other traditional fancy patterns; replace the crow's wing with mallard and you have a Mallard and Claret. The feature missing is the cheek of jungle cock, an item which would turn a dour pattern into a startling catcher of fish, but the jungle cock is a protected species, cultured feathers are both rare and expensive, and the use of enamel paint to emulate the 'eye' upsets the traditionalist. The fact that fly-tyers produce a pattern which is missing its most important feature is due to conservationists, who may have placed the future of the original Watson's Fancy in jeopardy, but, more importantly, may have ensured the survival of the jungle cock.

RIVER TROUT

Nymphs

Stoneflies

The Stonefly was of sufficient importance to be mentioned by name in the *Treatysse* and described at length by Cotton, but appears to have fallen from favour in the nineteenth century in much the same way as the March Brown. Most artificials in use are in the classic north country style of spider patterns fished wet to imitate both nymphal and adult forms; the *Willow Fly* (above) and Yellow Sally are good examples.

Again, it is a species found in the faster-flowing streams associated with the hillier parts of Britain, and whereas G.E.M. Skues, an angling entomologist who fished the southern chalkstreams, alludes to its appearance on the River Test following a flood in 1895, it was of no importance to the lowland angler. As a consequence, the stoneflies were largely ignored in contemporary literature which rather concentrated on the fashionable chalkstreams and use of the dry fly. However, the dry version of the Yellow Sally is a southern pattern.

Americans accord their freestone rivers the same respect that Europeans reserve for their chalkstreams, and take stoneflies, particularly in the nymphal form, very seriously. Dave Whitlock's *Stonefly Creeper* (centre) is such a pattern, as is Al Troth's Terrible Stone, both tied in the modern imitative style, while *Ted's Stonefly* (below), created by Ted Trueblood, has the impressionist look of a modified Montana Nymph.

Mayfly Nymphs

In May, when the weather has improved sufficiently to warm the water and the trout-fishing season is well under way, nature supplies the trout with the senior members of the upwinged flies, *Ephemera dancia* and *Ephemera vulgata*. These are the largest of British aquatic insects with a wingspan of nearly two inches, and anglers know them collectively as mayflies. Not all waters are suitable for these species – they require very pure water – and the hatches tend to be parochial; but the natural, where it does occur, represents a valuable food form. Nymphs encounter various difficulties and dangers during growth, but the mayfly, which spends the best part of its life underwater in a mud burrow, is most vulnerable when swimming erratically to the surface and whilst waiting beneath the surface film to hatch.

One of the best patterns to imitate the swimming larva is Richard Walker's Mayfly Nymph. This is illustrated here beside a variant, the *Stillborn Mayfly* (above), an unweighted, smooth-bodied version created to simulate a dead or dying natural.

The *Suspender Mayfly Nymph* (centre) borrows a technique from buzzer imitations which also have a ball of ethafoam, secured within a piece of stocking, to keep the artificial held in the surface film. The furry body represents the emerging nymph as it struggles for release from its shuck.

There is a very fine line between improvement and unnecessary interference with successful patterns. The variation of Walker's excellent imitation with plastic eyes (below) is a prime example of gilding the lily.

Dragons and Damsels

Dragonflies and damselflies are to be seen in their thousands above lakes at the height of summer, and whereas they are about the same size as craneflies, they must have a different taste, for in their adult form they are widely assumed to be of little interest to fish. The nymphal stage is another matter entirely, and the trout's appetite is matched by the angler's eagerness to imitate. The *Demoiselle* (above) is both popular and fairly simple, relying on a whisk to impart movement. Goddard's *Wiggle Nymph* (centre) is rather more complicated, using an articulated system developed in America by the Swisher-Richards team. The thorax is formed on one hook while the abdomen is tied to the shank of another. The two are attached by wire and the rearmost hook is sheared off. This affords the finished pattern a most alluring movement in water.

Authorities question the importance of the adult winged insect as a legitimate food form; some experienced anglers claim they have never seen fish take an adult damselfly. This is strange, for trout autopsies reveal their tastes to be catholic, including snails, flies, other fish, leeches and the occasional cigarette end. Not to feed on an insect of this size would seem to be a wasted opportunity, and it is in a spirit of optimism that the fly-fisher uses the *Adult Damselfly* (below). Blue is the obvious overall colour, and the long thorax the outstanding feature. Dyed deerhair, laid along the shank of a long hook and reaching beyond the bend, is the common method employed.

Bloodworms

The bloodworm is the larval stage of one of the chironomid family which, together with other members of the buzzer species, form a good part of a trout's diet. Bloodworms are generally found in the deeper zones of a lake or reservoir, but when the pumps and aerators are operating, they are churned up and rise to the surface, where a plausible artificial will be taken by an expectant fish.

The *Marabou Bloodworm* (above) uses peacock herl to create a standard buzzer-style head, behind which red floss silk forms a thin body; but it is marabou plume, tied in at the tail as an extension to the body which imparts lifelike movement to this pattern.

Dyed ostrich herl, ribbed with fine gold wire and a length of red feather fibres, creates a similar effect in the next *Bloodworm* illustrated (centre). Ostrich herl is the most delicate feather used in fly-tying and is eminently suitable for these small imitations.

Similar to Ivens's Green-and-Brown Nymph, but originating on the other side of the Atlantic, is the *Zugbug* (below), a general nymph pattern tied to represent any number of naturals, but similar to a dragonfly or damsel larva. The peacock-herl body is weighted with lead wire to reach fish feeding at depth, and it is another pattern to achieve good results on the small clearwater fisheries.

The Dry-Fly Fishing Revolution

In 1879, when Frederick Maurice Halford chanced to meet Captain George Selwyn Marryat in a Winchester tackle shop, a friendship began which was destined to change fly-fishing for ever. Halford, then aged forty-five, was to move to a house near Houghton Mill on the River Test the following year. The prescribed method of fishing the Test was the traditional wet fly, but Halford had already been introduced to, and captivated by, dry-fly fishing on a tributary of the Thames. He spent the next six years working with Marryat on the flora and fauna of chalkstreams, noting the natural insects and devising ways of tying artifiicals which would both float and be an accurate copy. The joint results were published under Halford's name in 1886. The methods advocated in *Floating Flies and How to Dress Them* spread like a bushfire. Basically, the concept was to cast upstream only to trout seen feeding on the surface. The fly used would be an exact imitation of the natural winged insect in which, by close observation, the fish was interested.

To suggest that Halford invented dry-fly fishing is, of course, nonsense: it simply evolved. But he undoubtedly revolutionised the technique. His ideas were embraced with enthusiasm, though unfortunately they were gradually converted into dogma. Halford himself may have become less flexible as he grew older – and his *Dry-Fly Fishing in Theory and Practice*, written in 1889, reflects the expansiveness of his observations and thoughts. Although few of his original patterns are fished today, their underlying theme is echoed in the vast majority of patterns which followed, together with their manner of use.

Frank Sawyer

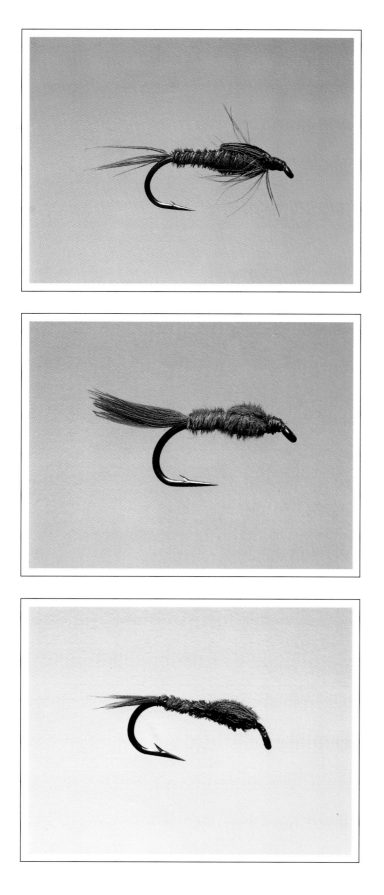

In 1928, Frank Sawyer began a career which was to span fifty-three years as river-keeper on a stretch of the River Avon in Hampshire's chalkstream country, much in the manner of William Lunn on the neighbouring Test. Whereas Lunn was contemporary of Halford, Sawyer had embraced the more expansive views of Skues, particularly in the way of nymph fishing, and his experience *in* as well as *on* the water led him to devise a general pattern which would sink quickly to the level of a targeted fish. Dispensing with the traditional tying silk, Sawyer used copper wire from a discarded electrical transformer to serve the dual purpose of forming a weighted underbody and securing the pheasant-tail herl from which his *Pheasant Tail Nymph* (above) is constructed. The pattern proved to be as successful on stillwaters as it was on rivers, imitating the darker olive and iron blue nymphs. By replacing the pheasant tail with grey goose fibres, he created the *Grey Goose Nymph* (centre), a good imitation of the pale watery and blue-winged olive nymphs. A quiet, unassuming man, Sawyer was held in high regard in influential fishing circles, not the least of whom was G.E.M. Skues, and he was the guest of HRH the Duke of Bavaria on several occasions.

The *SS Nymph* (below) was devised while visiting the lakes in the mountainous region of northern Sweden. Sawyer demonstrated to his hosts the value of both the Pheasant Tail and Grey Goose patterns, but one particular water proved to be something of an enigma, for the general patterns were being refused. Sawyer concentrated on capturing examples of the insect life rather than fish, and discovered that the trout were feeding not, as had previously been believed, on a species of March brown but on a larger, faster-swimming nymph. Out came the fly-tying materals and imitations were tied using large hooks in a similar style to the Grey Goose, but employing the darker primary wing feathers. To the delight of his hosts, success was both instant and remarkable; they suggested the name Sawyer's Swedish, later contracted to SS. In the event, this abbreviation was fortuitous for the insect which had so puzzled its captor was later identified as *Siphlonurus spinosus*, sometimes known as the summer mayfly. Despite its origin, the pattern travels well, for it has gained popularity on stillwaters in the UK as an imitation of larger olives and claret duns found in midsummer.

Arthur Cove

rthur Cove started fishing the great stillwaters more out of necessity than desire. Returning to England in 1952 after service in the army as Field Marshal Montgomery's driver, he discovered that very little river fishing was available around his home in the Midlands. He turned instead to Eyebrook reservoir, a 400-acre water modelled on a Scottish loch. Using traditional wet-fly techniques, he set about learning his trade. Undeterred by poor results, Cove employed keen observation of waterlife and inspection of the trout's stomach (much in the manner of Dr Bell at Blagdon) to conclude that 99 per cent of the trout's diet consisted of various nymphs and larvae. Suitable imitations were not available in the local tackle shops, so Cove bought a vice, thread and a few materials, and began to tie his own patterns from scratch. Fishing them improved his catch but, still unsatisfied, he studied the insects further in order to imitate their actual movements in the water. The resultant success, at a time when stillwater fishing was as yet in its infancy, is now legendary, as is the pattern which bears his name. *Cove's Pheasant Tail* (above) is very much in the impressionistic mould, and at first glance differs in that there is no tail, the body extends around the bend of the hook, and the thorax is dubbed rabbit's underfur.

Both the Cove and Sawyer nymphs have been subjected to variations, created by tying the body with swan feather dyed green, grey or black. Some are useful, others unsuccessful. However, one which combines the features of both originals is the *Orange Pheasant Tail Variant* (centre), a hybrid in which the rear half is

Sawyer's, the dubbed thorax (in this case orange seal's fur substitute) Cove's, with throat hackles added just for good measure.

Illustrated (right) is a detail of a typical pheasant tail feather.

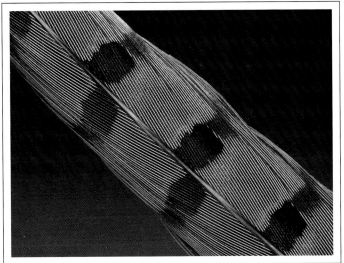

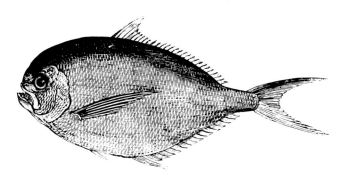

Water Boatmen and Freshwater Shrimps

The Corixidae are better known as water boatmen, and *Corixa punctata,* the lesser water boatman, is the most important species for stillwater anglers. The natural is predominantly brown, and is characterised by two long back legs which it uses to propel itself on or in the water. The underside is white, represented in the artificial with white floss. The natural swims to the surface to take in air which it holds as a bubble under the wings, and this feature is simulated by a winding of silver in the pattern. Imitations are tied in a manner which accurately reproduces the natural's swimming motion – a quick rise to the surface followed by a drifting descent – and this may be accomplished either by weighting the pattern with lead foil and using a floating line to draw the pattern to the surface, as in the case of the *Silver Corixa* (above), or by incorporating ethafoam for a buoyant pattern, such as the Plastazote Corixa.

Not all the naturals, however, are brown; the *Green Corixa* (centre) has a plump, rounded body tied with white fluorescent floss, ribbed with silver wire, and a green feather-fibre back. The traditional bearded hackle represents the legs of the natural which trail beneath the body on its journey to the surface.

The freshwater shrimp is a common sight along the freshwater margins, and it forms an important part of the trout's diet, particularly during the winter months when insect activity is scarce and food at a premium. The *Shrimper* (right) is an effective imitation which captures the principal features of the natural. A copper wire underbody adds weight and forms the familiar hump, over which is wound a dubbing of olive-brown seal's fur (or substitute) and a palmered hackle, both serving to copy the shrimp's numerous legs. Clear polythene is stretched across the back and copper wire secures, protects and gives the impression of the body segments.

Collyer and Welham Nymphs

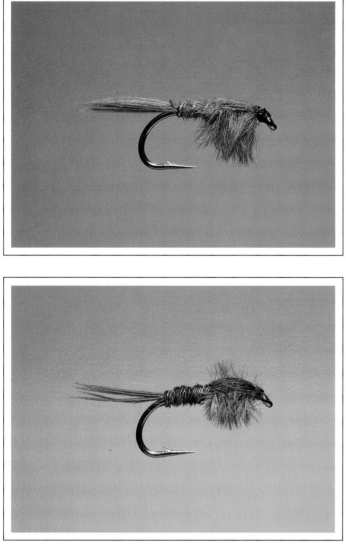

David Collyer's series of nymphs utilise a wider range of materials than the patterns of Sawyer and Cove, which relied solely on pheasant tail fibres. Softer feathers, such as swan and heron, are used, and the fur thorax is replaced with ostrich herl dyed the same colour as the abdomen and tail.

The most popular versions are the *Green Collyer Nymph* (above) and the *Brown Collyer Nymph* (centre), successful general patterns fished along the margins and weedbanks of the stillwater in which Collyer discovered the naturals on which he based his designs.

The *Barry Welham Nymph* (below) was devised in the 1960s as a stalking pattern for the small clearwater lakes of southern England. Most of the nymph patterns for this type of water are heavily weighted because the waters are deep and the artificial must sink quickly to intercept a cruising trout, but Welham required a slow-sinking pattern for fish roving closer to the surface. The pattern is based on another stillwater nymph, the Brown Woolly, but it is purely coincidental that this variant was developed by a tyer with the same initials. The bulky brown body aids buoyancy while the short fluorescent tail adds to its attraction. The breathing filaments, similar to those on the Buzzer imitations, were originally white hackle fibres, although white fluorescent floss is frequently substituted.

Nymph Patterns

The *Stickfly* (above) is very popular in Britain as a stillwater pattern. There are many versions of this caddis larva imitation, all of which should ideally be fished along the bottom, although it seems to be fished at all levels and at all speeds with equal success. It is a very satisfactory general pattern which catches trout in all conditions. It may be tied with lead wire for bottom fishing or unweighted as a general nymph pattern. The body is either peacock herl or turkey feather, but a ginger hackle is universal.

Alan Pearson's *Twitchitt Nymph* (centre) is very similar but uses a body of cock pheasant tail fibres, as in the Pheasant Tail Nymph, but with a thorax of grey rabbit fur over a copper underbody.

The effect of DFM (daylight fluorescent material) floss is seen in the *Darker Twitchitt Nymph* (below) which emulates the conditions to be found in deeper, coloured water. Although the rest of the pattern is hardly visible, the DFM tag shines out like a beacon to catch the attention of distant fish.

Dapping

Dapping is a method of angling which predates the Edwardian dry-fly techniques by several centuries – indeed it is probably the oldest known fly-fishing tradition.

The accepted style requires a large expanse of water, a boat, a long rod and a good breeze. The conventional fly-fishing line is abandoned in favour of a length of woven monofilament, although horsehair would have been used in bygone days, to which is attached a dapping fly. The rod is raised and the wind catches both fly and line, which is gradually paid out until sufficient has been relaeased for the fly to touch the surface. The effect of the wind catching the line, coupled with the lifting and lowering of the rod tip, causes the fly to rise and fall on the waves in a manner which fish find most enticing. The takes are quite dramatic as the fish will frequently leap above the surface, and the method makes an exciting and popular pastime for novices and experienced anglers alike.

The pattern used for dapping is unimportant – most are fairly nondescript – but the technique favours large, bushy, palmered patterns which are blown about by the wind. Most of them come from Ireland and lough-fishers customarily fish the more imitative patterns, such as the Mayfly and Daddy-Long-Legs.

A derivation of the method is sometimes used by fly-fishers confronted by a bankside heavily overgrown with trees and bushes. Here the solution is to tie on a heavily dressed pattern with a weight above, and to poke it through the foliage. The rod is then gently lowered and raised to simulate a hovering insect.

Plastic Nymph Patterns

It may be said that the first part of the twentieth century saw the creation of the modern nymph shape – long, slim and tapering towards the tail – and that it was Skues who set the fashion. The next step was to match the coloration of the natural, and this was soon evident in various tyings. Close observers realised that the skin of the larvae created a translucent shell around the natural's body, an aspect never addressed in the fur- or feather-bodied patterns, and set about the problem with gusto. The common plastic bag is the source of the overbody in John Goddard's *PVC Nymph* (above), an excellent representation of the lake and pond olives. The material may not look particularly clear, but when stretched to breaking point, a strip will not only halve its width but will also become very transparent. This nymph pattern is not unlike Sawyer's Pheasant Tail: it is weighted, has a tail, abdomen, swollen thorax, and a wing-case of folded pheasant-tail herl. But the principal material is olive condor herl (the substitute is dyed goose wing) and the abdomen is overwound with the prestretched PVC. It is an excellent companion pattern to the Pheasant Tail Nymph.

Whereas PVC may add the required translucency it does not effectively mimic the body segments present in some species of nymphs and larvae. Traditionally, fine wire is wrapped in a spiral over the body material to achieve both strength and a suitable impression; but tyers were soon searching the vast range of plastics for new ideas.

Swannundaze is a plastic strip, flat one side and curved the other, and available in a wide choice of colours, ideally suited to the job. It is American in origin, introduced by Frank Johnson, and blends well with other materials, as illustrated by the *Swannundaze Stonefly Larva* (centre).

By wrapping clear polythene over an under-body of silver tinsel, Ken Sinfoil obtained the degree of translucency he required for his elegant fry imitator, the *Sinfoil's Fry* (right). He is credited as the first in Britain to use polythene for fly-tying.

Buzzers

Fishing with midge patterns is probably more popular in the United States than in Britain, where it seems to be the province of the stillwater fly-fisher, who tends to imitate the pupal stage of what the Americans call *buzzers*, a larger species of insect so named because of the annoying noise they make. But the term *midge* is correctly applied to describe a broad spectrum of tiny insects, from the relatively substantial large green midge down to the minute small black midge. Stillwater fly-fishers have addressed the problem of imitating this group quite successfully, but the river fisher has traditionally ignored their increasing importance – increasing because with endemic pollution in rivers, the upwinged species are disappearing in favour of the midges. The *Suspender Midge Pupa* (above) from Goddard utilises an ethafoam ball which serves the dual purpose of ensuring the pattern floats hook downwards in the surface film whilst caricaturing the white breathing gills of the natural. This pattern, probably originating in the United States, could be called impressionistic, but the alternatives, tied with tufts of white wool or silk floss at the head and tail, such as the Hatching Midge Pupa, are more specifically imitative.

The dressings are tied around the hook bend to copy the curve of the natural and all the patterns are ribbed to the body segments. Peacock feather invariably forms the head. In the *Black Midge Pupa* (centre), ostrich feather is used

as a body material, white wool is tied in above the head to represent the breathing filaments and white floss for the tail filaments. The *Green Midge Pupa* (right) relies on the tying silk alone to form a smoother body, the ribbing is fine brass wire and white wool represents the filaments.

Buzzers

The natural pupa has a translucent body which may be represented by overwinding the pattern with clear, prestretched polythene before tying in the peacock-herl head. The underbody of floss silk, ribbed with flat silver tinsel, looks very realistic. The accepted method of fishing these patterns is to grease the monofilament leader to within a couple of inches of the nymph, causing the line to float and the patterns to sink just below the surface. Apart from the occasional twitch to add the smallest movement, the patterns are fished static.

The transformation of pupa into adult, with the tiny wings of the natural copied and the throat hackles simulating the legs, is represented in the Hatching Buzzer. The patterns illustrated are used at Blagdon Lake. The *Blagdon Green Midge* (above), fished close to the surface, accurately resembles the hatching winged insect. Chironomids appear in various colours – green, black, olive, red, silver and orange are all common – and the artificials are similarly tied in a range of colours and sizes, for only by trial and error will the fly-fisher discover the correct combination. Examples illustrated are the *Black Hatching Buzzer* (centre) and the *Red Hatching Buzzer* (below), tied with brown whisks to represent the legs.

Chompers

Chompers are a series of very simple, yet most effective, patterns. One cannot call them nymphs, nor are they flies, for they are representative of a variety of aquatic food forms. Their success is partly attributable to their ease of tying; indeed, tyro fly-tyers are usually advised to tie a Black Peacock Spider first and then move on to the Chompers. There are only two component parts to a Chomper – the body, formed by winding ostrich herl along the hookshank, and, stretched over it, a back of raffene, a plastic raffia substitute available in a multitude of colours. By altering the colours of both body and backing, and adding weight in the form of a lead underbody, a variety of food forms are imitated, albeit in an impressionistic sense; black versions serve well as beetle imitations, green can simulate olive nymphs or, tied in large sizes with peacock herl substituted for ostrich, a passable dragonfly nymph is created. Examples illustrated are the *Green Chomper* (above), *White Chomper* (centre) and *Orange Chomper* (below). The last version, along with the Buff Chomper, is a shrimp pattern with the additional allure of the colour which fish seem to find so attractive. In much the same way as the afore-mentioned Wulff patterns, opportunities are limited only by the imagination of the tyer – so in that sense there is no such animal as a bad Chomper pattern.

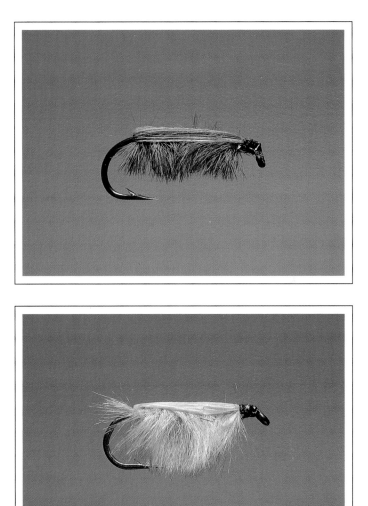

Lumphs

The *Persuader* (above) is a departure from the usual patterns of John Goddard for it has the proportions of a modern nymph pattern but the coloration of a lure. It was designed to tempt trout to rise on large still-waters in dour conditions, and it fulfils the original requirements for such a pattern – that it should be large and of a highly visible colour, yet retaining the dimensions of a food form. The thorax of seal's fur and wing cases of brown turkey are similar to those of the Amber Nymph, another successful pattern, but the translucent body created by ostrich herl is novel. The Persuader may be tied weighted for fast retrieval just beneath the surface, in the manner of a lure. The weighted version is also ideal for targeting the large trout of the spring-fed clear-water lakes – these waters are deceptively deep and require a pattern which will sink rapidly to the level of a cruising fish. So is the Persuader a nymph or a lure? Perhaps it belongs to a category of its own – *Lumph*.

Another contender for the lumph classification is the *Montana Nymph* (centre), from that American state. It is in a similar mould to other North American stonefly patterns, but when it was imported to Britain by the Orvis Company, reservoir anglers were quick to adopt it as a lure. The Montana is a chenille pattern, black for the body and yellow for the thorax. The latter has a black cock hackle wound through, and the short tail of black hackle tips is more imitative than lurelike.

The success of the original has spawned variations in which the thorax colour changes either to green or red; but the *Montana Variant* illustrated (below) has altered the entire overall look of the original and should properly be renamed. This is a reservoir lure in which the thorax has disappeared, the palmering has moved to the body and the round head is likewise yellow. A longer marabou tail replaces the original to create more movement.

RIVER TROUT

Lures

Beetles and Bugs

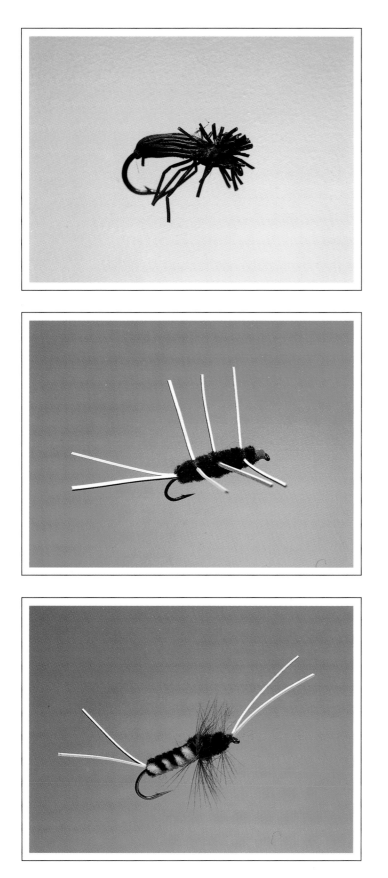

The *Black Deerhair Beetle* (above) may be used to imitate the majority of beetle species, of which there are tens of thousands. Whereas an elementary grasp of entomology is valuable to the fly-fisher, identifying the exact species of these small beetles which are blown on to the water is unnecessary, and most anglers are content with general imitations. In the dog days of summer when it is too hot for aquatic insects to hatch, the torpid trout may well be tempted by a beetle imitation which plops on to the surface. The deerhair pattern is both quick and easy to tie: a bunch of fibres is tied in at the bend, doubled over and tied off in the usual manner. The cellular structure of deerhair makes this pattern virtually unsinkable.

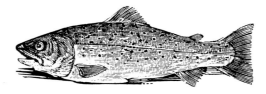

The *Girdle Bug* (centre) is an American approach to beetle mimicry, using a chenille body and rubber legs, the source of which was the elastic from a popular foundation garment. The marvellous thing about this elastic is its capacity for retaining its shape in water whilst yielding readily to pressure from the jaws of a fish. This unique material has been utilised to good effect in a derivation of the celebrated Montana Nymph called the *Bitch Creek* (below); conveniently, manufacturers are now supplying this elastic in various forms, including an all-black type.

Ivens's Spiders

When Tom C. Ivens wrote *Still Water Fly Fishing*, published in 1952, it was to become the bible of British still-water anglers for two decades. His *Black and Peacock Spider* (above) is a derivation of the Alder, for Ivens was fishing that pattern without luck until he cut off the wings to create this novelty. Still very much in vogue today, the Black and Peacock is probably taken for a beetle or snail. Some of its popularity must be attributed to the ease of tying, an essential ingredient for a pattern's prosperity. The *Jersey Herd* (centre) is his successful lure tied to imitate fry. Channel Islands milk, from Jersey and Guernsey cows, was bottled with a gold-coloured top, and Ivens used that metal foil for the wide body-ribbing of this pattern, hence the name. Again, Ivens's series of nymphs are both easy to tie and effective imitations of the sedge pupa. They are tied with peacock-herl heads and variously coloured bodies to create the Brown, Green, Green-and-Yellow and, perhaps the most famous, *Green-and-Brown* (below).

Richard Walker

Richard Walker influenced the 1960s as Ivens had the 1950s, creating patterns used both by stillwater and river fly-fishers. His *Mayfly Nymph* (above) is probably the most commonly used pattern to represent the natural. It has an underbody of lead over-wound with the palest of pale yellow angora wool. Pheasant tail fibres form the tail, wing cases and whisks, while the body is finished with varnish applied to the top and underside.

The *Mrs Palmer* (centre) was devised by Walker as an end-of-season pattern in 1973. The original tying used jungle cock feathers to form a cheek, as seen in so many of the Victorian and Edwardian traditional wet flies, but the use of goat's hair as a winging material – he considered goat to have more mobility than bucktail in water – and the long slim body of white fluores-cent wool testify to its more recent origins. In the example illustrated, the jungle cock cheeks have been omitted – the feathers are rare – but the yellow colouring of the goathair wing has been augmented to compensate. It is not unlike a salmon fly – perhaps he noted their methods of fishing coloured (muddied) waters – for that is precisely when the Mrs Palmer is most effective.

The *Polystickle* (right) is a fry imitator also attributed to Walker, although to be fair he originated the Sticklefly, and another tyer, Ken Sinfoil, added an overbody of polythene strip to give translucency, calling the revised pattern the Polystickle. It is a lake pattern used to imitate the stickleback, a small fish with spines on its back. At the end of the season, when lake trout crash into shoals of their tiny cousins – a practice known as *fry-bashing* – this pattern comes into its own. A derivation of the pattern, the Glow-stickle, utilises a luminous plastic strip beneath the polythene body to add glow-in-the-dark attraction for deepwater or night fishing. Similar ideas have been mooted for sea trout fishing, and presumably we shall soon see the incorporation of the coarse angler's float lights – small plastic tubes filled with a glowing chemical, activated by bending the tube and used to enable anglers to see a float at night – into simple patterns. High-tech but low-aesthetic.

Fish Fry Imitations

The cannibalistic nature of the trout is especially pronounced near the end of the season when their breeding instincts and aggression reach their peak. On the large stillwaters they will rush towards the shoreline, frequently in considerable numbers, crashing into the densely packed shoals of small fish fry to be found in the margins. Not only are individual small fish successfully chased and caught, but they are often stunned and left to float to the surface to be devoured at leisure. Bob Church, a Northampton reservoir angler, tied his *Church Fry* (above) in 1963, and it became very popular following publicity by Dick Walker. The American techniques, which Church was quick to recognise and embrace, are very apparent in the hairwing style, although some may question the use of an orange body to imitate the perch fry. However, this makes the artificial stand out from the naturals and the use and evident success of orange or red in late-season patterns is well known. The Church Fry, still as popular as ever, was to set the standard of innovative patterns from the Church stable.

The *Whisky Fly* (centre) was devised by Albert Whillock in the 1970s as a reservoir pattern. When fished moderately close to the surface, it attracts rainbow trout, probably because it imitates a fish fry, but part of its success must be attributable to its mixture of bright colour – often fluorescent – and the mobility of the hairwing. It is a combination which scores heavily in muddied waters.

The *Missionary* (right) is a fry imitator which looks similar to the Matuka style from New Zealand. This is rather confusing, as one Captain J.J. Dunn is credited with its invention for use on Blagdon Lake in Somerset, England. However, the version illustrated, which uses a complete teal feather laid flat over the hook's length, is attributed to Dick Shrine.

Threads

The foundation of any artificial pattern is the thread with which it is tied, and there is a wide selection to cater for different techniques. The traditional thread was silk, available in three types: *Gossamer*, a fine grade for the smallest patterns, *Naples*, a thicker, stronger thread for larger lures and salmon flies, and *Marabou*, a floss silk twisted in a double strand and used for constructing wound bodies and some tags. Unfortunately, silk will rot if allowed to remain damp, and the thread had to be pulled across a piece of hard cobbler's wax or beeswax, which acted as a preservative.

When terylene thread became available, it was the obvious choice for fly-tyers; not only is it stronger than silk but it lies flatter when wound around the hook, making a smoother foundation for body and hackle. Although this man-made fibre is not prone to rotting, wax is still used to form a slightly tacky surface, which aids the application of dubbing materials, and thus modern specialist threads are supplied prewaxed. Again, various strengths are available, the heaviest of which is necessary when applying the spun deerhair techniques. Rayon or acetate have replaced silk marabou and come wound in four strands, only one strand being used at a time.

Colours are many and varied, but an important step has been the introduction of fluorescent acetate floss, adding extra attraction to wet patterns and lures, although since their effect is reliant upon ultraviolet rays which only penetrate the first few feet of water, their suitability on lures which are designed to be fished deep is questionable. But their use in patterns that contain orange or red is universally popular.

Dogs and Barbers

Dog hair is an easy source of material for the tyer, and Harry Powell used the hair from a mongrel sheepdog to tie his patterns the *Dogsbody* (above), in 1924. It has been suggested that this dry fly mimics the sandfly but it is more properly a general imitation effective when gnats, olives, iron blues and the like are on the water.

Since tying and selling flies was insufficient to make a living, Harry Powell supplemented his income by turning to another professional skill – hairdressing. If this conjures up images of the Demon Barber of Fleet Street, it is perhaps comforting to realise that human hair, one of few to have no taper, is in any event too soft for use in fly-tying. Yet, in this somewhat sinister context, it is worth recalling that Dick Walker devised a lure pattern with a difference. Black is possibly the most versatile colour for lures since it catches fish at all levels. But lures are long and this is sometimes a drawback, causing the fish to *take short* – that is, nip the tail and miss the hook, particularly if the tail is long. In order to solve the problem, Walker moved the red tag from the tail position to the throat, and it certainly worked. With black humour, he named the pattern *Sweeney Todd* (below), reflecting the cut-throat look. Donald Overfield's Appendix to Courtney Williams's *Dictionary of Trout Flies* mentions a two-hook tandem version of this pattern, measuring two-and-a-half inches, presumably for loch-style fishing.

Fish Fry Imitations

Tinsels and wires used in early patterns were metal and suffered from tarnishing, particularly when fished in saltwater. The plastics industry changed all that. Mylar, whilst affording less protection from sharp teeth, remains bright and shining regardless of use. When it became available as a woven tube, tyers were quick to realise that it closely imitated the scales of a fish and set about creating new patterns and modifying their favourites. Syd Brock's *Mylar Minnow* (above) incorporates a body of mylar tubing with a traditional back of peacock herl to give the unmistakable look of a small fish.

Ethafoam is likewise a modern material which, unlike the beaded expanded polystyrene, is pliable enough to form a thin malleable sheet. The attraction of mylar and the buoyancy of ethafoam have combined to produce the *Floating Fry* (centre), a surface pattern used to imitate a dead or dying fry.

The *Darter* (below) incorporates the mylar body and the peacock-herl head (as a whisk), but a wing is added, streamer style, to enhance the pattern.

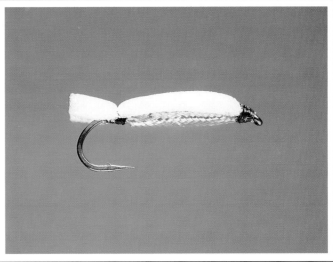

Nobblers

Marabou is a particularly soft, fluffy feather which moves well in water. The common substitutes, feathers from the inside of a turkey's leg, is used to good effect in the Dog Nobbler series by Trevor Houseby, introduced in the early 1980s to create a lure which would appeal to the wily larger trout he nicknamed *dogs*. The patterns are tied on long-shanked hooks weighted at the eye, which allows the lure to sink in the water before rising again on the retrieve. The body is formed of chenille wound over lead wire, the colour matching the feathered tail, and all have a peacock-herl head. Halford would not have approved – indeed, many contemporary anglers dislike their use, but none can doubt their effectiveness. It may be argued that the *Olive Dog Nobbler* (above) represents the damselfly nymph, whilst the *Black Dog Nobbler* (centre) could be taken for a leech, but the Pink (shocking pink at that) cannot lay claim to any imitation whatsoever, relying on shock tactics to induce a take. The Orange version is popular during the summer when trout in greenish water seem to find orange lures particularly attractive.

Bob Church utilised the marabou tail with a body of mylar tube (plaited mylar, which has a similar appearance to the scales of a fish) to create the Frog Nobbler series. This style has been popular since it proved a success in an international fishing competition against the French, hence its name. The addition of painted eyes and a hackle makes the Black and Green Frog Nobbler an attractive fry imitation; and turkey feathers are readily available. Rather than using lead at the head to cause the pattern to sink, lateral thinking has created the *Booby* (right), similar to the Dog Nobbler but utilising the ethafoam ball wrapped in stocking to form eyes, a method previously seen in the Suspender Midge.

Black and White

There are plenty of black lures in the stillwater fly-fisher's armoury, but few can boast the consistent success of the *Viva* (above), a black chenille lure. The hairwing shown in the pattern illustrated may be replaced with marabou – possibly the extra movement imparted would be an asset when fished slowly – but it is the green fluorescent tag that sets this pattern apart from the crowd, and it was to become a feature of others which followed. The smallest patterns are the size of a traditional loch fly but the largest would match a salmon fly.

The *Nailer* (centre) is a big, long-shanked reservoir lure devised by Dick Shrive in the 1950s. Dark oak turkey feathers are tied along each side of the red cock-feather wing, and the shank is covered with gold lurex or tinsel ribbed with gold wire. An alternative tying is to use goat's hair, creating an artificial not unlike the modern salmon and sea trout patterns. Authorities are divided as to its method of use, some contending that it is a pattern for fishing deep on a sinking line, while others recommend a floating line, with the pattern fished close to the surface to represent the sedge.

Almost a decade after his now famous Church Fry, Bob Church introduced another fry imitator, the *Appetiser* (right). In 1972, this pattern was truly imitative for a British lure, combining the American styles and materials which so influenced its creator. The body is white chenille ribbed with silver tinsel. Chenille, easier to use than dubbing, quickly creates an even, robust body. The beard hackle utilises green and yellow feather fibres mixed with silver mallard and this is repeated at the tail. The wing is a combination of white marabou feathers (possibly the first British pattern to do so) and grey squirrel.

Muddlers

There are plenty of patterns which imitate fry, and many others which simulate sedges, but the Muddler is a pattern that may be used to represent either, although principally the former. The original Mudler Minnow, an American pattern devised by Don Gapen in 1953, makes use of the buoyant properties of deerhair. The hair is spun around the hookshank in a series of turns, packed tightly and trimmed. The wing is grey squirrel hair between two oak turkey wing slips. The tail utilises the same feather.

Reservoir anglers embraced the idea enthusiastically, particularly in the Midlands, and created both the *Black Muddler* (above) and the *White Muddler* (centre). The shape of the head has been altered since the original was introduced in 1967, with bullet, cone and ball shapes commonly available, but Gapen's concept remains the same.

The incorporation of another popular material, marabou, gives the wing more movement in the water and consequently the pattern more life. Orange is a preferred colour for lures in coloured or cloudy water, and mylar effectively represents fish scales. The two are combined in the *Orange Marabou Muddler.*

New Zealand Patterns

The 1970s saw the introduction of a style of tying from New Zealand which uses a single feather tied to the hookshank in the manner of a dorsal fin. The style takes its name from the bird which originally supplied the feathers, the matuka, and the method was introduced to Britain by John Veniard and David Collyer, who devised the now-famous *Ace of Spades* (above). Long feathers such as marabou are frequently called for in the construction of lures, where their mobility in water adds the necessary life to a pattern. The drawback with long feathers is that they are inclined to wrap around the leader during casting, but this problem is overcome in the Matuka styles. Fibres are stripped from one side of the feather and the bare quill is placed on the hookshank and tied with thread and/or ribbing, leaving the unstripped tip to lie beyond the bend to form a tail. The resultant pattern has all the movement of the long-feathered patterns but retrieves on a very even keel, is tangle free and much stronger.

Another pattern from New Zealand to achieve international recognition is a lure called *Mrs Simpson* (centre) which, in a style similar to the Matukas, utilises whole feathers – in this case brown partridge (below) – to create a fin-shaped wing. However, unlike the Matuka, this pattern employs four feathers of different lengths which overlap to form a bulkier fly. The underbody is chenille.

Ghosts and Christmas Trees

The _Christmas Tree_ (above) is an aptly named lure, combining the three most popular colours, black, red and green, in a concoction which proved itself on the large Midland reservoir, Rutland Water. The original, tied by Les Lewis, was used as the basis of a tandem version by Steve Parton for boat fishing on the same water. It is perhaps the very epitome of the modern lure, relying as it does on marabou, fluorescent floss and chenille.

During the 1960s, Bob Church and a few others were avid readers of the American angling press, which produces magazines of such high quality that the British equivalents pale by comparison. The American streamer patterns were quickly put into use on the large reservoirs which were becoming increasingly important to the fly-fisher on an overcrowded island. The lures used today have their origins in the American streamers, of which the _Gray Ghost_ (centre), devised in 1924 by Mrs Carrie G. Stevens, is both a classic and beautiful example. With the proliferation of large lures in use today, one must look back to the traditional wet winged patterns to realise just what an impact they must have made at the time. Interestingly enough, streamers are still employed for river fishing in North America whereas their use is restricted in Britain to stillwaters.

Tup's Indispensable

The Tup's claim to fame owes less to its undeniable effectiveness than to its rather peculiar dressing.

R.S. Austin was a professional fly-tyer and tobacconist based in Tiverton, Devon. Late in the season of 1900, he sent a sample of dubbing to G.E.M. Skues with instructions for tying an unnamed pattern which he had found to be a successful imitation of a female olive spinner. Accounts of Skues's experiments that same September and his success the following year on the River Itchen were duly published, and a star was born. Skues himself eventually named the fly and suggested the addition of a little crimson seal's fur; but by keeping the dubbing ingredients a close secret, Austin ensured a monopoly, initially for himself and, after his death in 1911, for his daughter.

Eventually the secret was published. It transpired that the body-fur comprised a mixture of white wool from a ram's scrotum, lemon-coloured fur from a spaniel, and a little yellow mohair, replaced by the crimson seal's fur recommended by Skues. The yellow tying silk is exposed as a thorax at the rear, and yellow-spangled light blue cock hackles are used for tail and hackle.

Austin's choice of such strange material (not novel but in this context associated exclusively with him) may be explained by the fact that he lived in sheep country and must often have watched farmers bringing the animals and their fleeces to market. Mackintosh describes the wool in question as 'a beautiful dusty yellow' – presumably dyed that colour indelibly by urine. When dampened, the colour deepens.

Baby Dolls

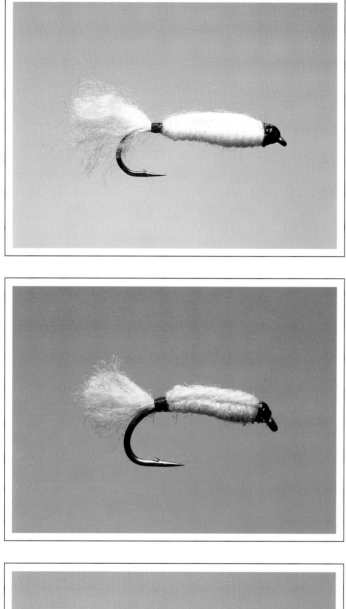

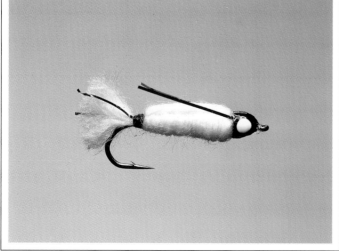

The *Baby Doll* (above), created in 1971 by Brian Kench, is a stillwater lure which tempts trout with white baby wool. It has proved as attractive to reservoir fish as it is to mothers, and although the original pattern was all white, the variations include the addition of a coloured back and tail of pink, green, orange or red.

In most forms the Baby Doll may be taken as a fry imitation, although it is hardly an accurate representation of the original. It raises again the arguments for and against mimicking a food which is of comparatively minor importance in the overall diet of a trout, for whilst it may be true to say that as many as 80 per cent of the fish taken on reservoirs and large stillwaters are caught on lures, many of which purport to be imitations of small fish, very few of these trout have fry in their stomachs. This leads to the conclusion that lures are taken for other reasons than being confused with food forms. Brian Clarke, a master of piscatorial reasoning, goes so far as to suggest that the closer one tries to imitate fish fry, the less successful they will prove. But since he published his argument in *The Pursuit of Stillwater Trout* in 1975, fry patterns have become more realistic and, moreover, are enjoying success which reinforces his original argument that fish take these patterns for motives other than greed. With the exception of tadpoles, no fish fry are black, yet black lures are effective, including a version of the Baby Doll, aptly named The Undertaker.

The *Peach Baby Doll* (centre) is considered to be effective when plankton and algae colour the water with a greenish hue; the lures frequently utilise orange or peach to overcome this problem. The addition of a little red tinsel and white painted eyes produces the *Gollidoll* (below).

SEA TROUT

Teal Series

Hugh Falkus

The Teal, Blue and Silver, that nineteenth-century favourite for loch-style fishing of trout and sea trout, is the basis for Hugh Falkus's *Medicine Fly* (above). Mr Falkus, generally acknowledged as the leading authority on sea trout in the United Kingdom, is very much a practical tyer and simplicity is the essence of this pattern. Contrary to many commercially tied versions of the Medicine, the correct tying dispenses with the oval silver body, preferring instead a flat silver one or just a coating of silver paint, and the wings should be of widgeon until autumn, when mallard is substituted. The finished fly should give an impression of slimness, enhanced by a lightweight hook, and it represents pinfry, those tiny fish which bigger species find so appetising.

If a larger version is required, Falkus insists on tube-fly tying, whereby the materials are tied around a plastic tube through which the line is passed before attachment to a treble hook. The force of water ensures that the hook and tube are presented as one, but when the fish takes, the tube is free to slide beyond the hook, denying the hooked fish the benefit of leverage against a shank.

The *Sunk Lure* (centre) is a tandem version of the Medicine, used at night. The wing feather is replaced by a blue cock hackle and a few strands of peacock herl, the whole apparatus trailing well behind the hook. In the example illustrated, the two hooks are joined with nylon braid, not only stronger than monofilament but, since the hookshank is inserted into the braid prior to tying, far more secure.

One of the frustrating problems associated with the use of long-winged patterns is that of the fish taking short – chasing after the fly without actually hooking itself. This becomes even more likely when maggots are attached to the lure. Falkus designed his *Secret Weapon* (right) to overcome such a situation. It is a fairly simple pattern with a brown seal's fur body, mallard wing and brown hackle; but fixed rigidly behind on a loop of strong monofilament is a treble hook from which the quarry is unlikely to escape.

The Falkus patterns are devised solely for the pursuit of sea trout, a migratory fish which, like the salmon, returns from the sea to breed in the upper reaches of a river. Sea trout are shy, resting during the daylight hours and continuing their journey at night, the most rewarding time for anglers. They make a splendid quarry, certainly worthy of the modern specialist patterns.

Winged Wets

By the middle of the nineteenth century, the wet patterns (many of which are still in use) were firmly established as the accepted method of fishing the great rivers, lochs and lakes. They seemed to fall into two broad categories: the winged style, many of which originated on the Scottish lochs, and the spider patterns associated (though by no means exclusively) with the northern English streams. Of the winged wets, some were vaguely imitative while others were simply attractor patterns.

The *Teal, Blue and Silver* (above) is one of a series of early nineteenth-century Scottish flies used loch-style for sea trout and salmon. In some variations the tail of golden pheasant tippet feathers – something of a trait among the winged wets – is retained along with the wings from a teal's breast feather (examples centre), but the body fur is changed to create the Teal and Red, Teal and Black and *Teal and Green* (below).

SALMON

Rare Feathers

Durham Ranger & Elver Fly

The *Durham Ranger* (above), which is thought to have been the first pattern to include jungle-cock feathers, began life with a bang. Its originator, Mr Scruton, cast his new fly into the Tweed and hooked a thirty-pound fish, ensuring a successful trip and certain popularity for his pattern. James Wright used the original to create the almost inevitable series of coloured variants: Blue, Black, Red, Orange and Silver.

Arthur Ransome is doubtless better known for his fictional works, such as *Swallows and Amazons*, than for his piscatorial pursuits, but he was as adept with rod as with pen and gave us the *Elver Fly* (below), a salmon and sea trout pattern loosely based on the eels with which the Atlantic salmon is associated. The elverine eel is found in the river estuaries and forms a nutritious final meal for salmon returning to the rivers of their birth to breed. It is believed that the adult salmon feeds only in saltwater and fasts on its journey to the redds, the gravel-bottomed areas of river in which it lays its eggs. The beautifully marked and slender blue feathers of the vulturine guinea fowl are an intrinsic component of this pattern and much sought by tyers. Fortunately, birds are now bred in captivity for the sole purpose of harvesting these rather expensive feathers.

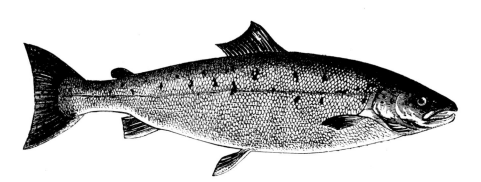

Doctors

The origin of the Doctor series is lost in the mists of time, but the original, the Blue Doctor, probably goes back to the beginning of the nineteenth century, possibly in Ireland. The celebrated tyer James Wright produced his own versions, and others, including Messrs Hardy, the Pall Mall tacklists, have added to the series. As with so many of the early salmon flies complicated tyings which presented no problems when labour was cheap and plentiful have become more simple over the years, as exemplified by the *Black Doctor* (above) and *Silver Doctor* (below).

This hairwing style is not new – a few salmon patterns were tied with hairwings in Britain over a century ago – but the norm was for bright, heavily dressed feather patterns. Not until the introduction of the greased line technique for low-water conditions in the present century did the salmon fisher become aware that simple patterns were just as effective. Consequently, American hairwing techniques and materials were imported and the traditional patterns adapted. Looking at a fully dressed salmon fly, this would appear to be an impossible task, but it is the colour combination which is all-important, and these are retained in the modern style of dressing.

The Jock Scott, Mar Lodge & Yellow Torrish

The *Jock Scott* (above) is named after its Scottish inventor and dates from the middle of the nineteenth century. The full list of feathers required might bore the casual reader but apart from jungle cock (which first appeared on the Durham Ranger and was obviously beginning a trend), some of the more fascinating items are speckled bustard, florican, six toucan feathers, white-tipped turkey and blue-and-yellow macaw – imagine the time needed to gather such material.

The *Mar Lodge* (centre) is a fly of the River Dee in Aberdeenshire, Scotland, named after the royal hunting lodge. That it has survived a century of change in the styles of salmon-fly dressing marks it as a classic, although one can only wonder at how few of these patterns are actually used for fishing, since the Mar Lodge requires no less than thirteen different types of feather and double that number of component parts.

The *Yellow Torrish* (right) is another fancy pattern, as effective at catching the eye of an angler passing the tackle shop. However, as with so many of these patterns, only time will tell if they endure the advent of the tube and *Waddington* style of dressing (the Torrish has been adapted for the newer, easier style). It would be nice to think that a few purists will ensure the line survives. Fully dressed traditional salmon flies are still fished today, albeit by avid enthusiasts. More importantly, they are still being tied commercially and framed collections for gracing the wall may be obtained through good gamefishing retailers. It does seem a fitting display for such beautiful creations.

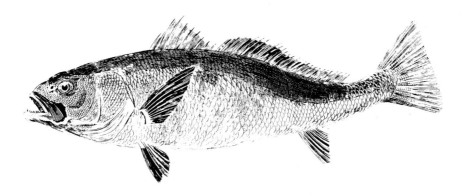

Shrimps and Prawns

Shrimps and prawns are high on the salmon's list of comestibles, a fact which has not passed unnoticed by anglers worldwide, so these lowly creatures have dozens, even hundreds, of imitations, although most of the patterns simulate the colour of a boiled prawn. Just why a wild salmon should be attracted to a culinary delight is a mystery, but the colouring seems to work.

The *General Practitioner* (above) was tied in 1953 by Lt-Col. Esmond Drury to overcome a ban on natural bait while fishing the River Test in Hampshire. It is as effective now as it was then.

Similar to the General Practitioner is the *Shrimp* (centre). Once again, the outstanding feature is a clump of golden pheasant tippet feathers, over which is swept a white hackle. Ginger feather fibres form the tail, if it could be so described, for these patterns are tied back to front.

This last feature is even more apparent in Peter Deane's imitative *Yellow Francis* (below), named after a lady who was preoccupied with tying Deane's successful patterns. Tied on a double hook, the tapered body is yellow wool palmered with a ginger hackle and ribbed with wire. The whiskers are a combination of stripped hackle stems and pheasant tail fibres, and the novel imitation is completed with plastic bead eyes.

GRAYLING

Fancy Patterns

Grayling Patterns

Trout must compete with other fish, many of them coarse fish which are considered to be poor sport by the game-fisher. However, the grayling, sometimes known as the fourth gamefish, is both a respected and welcome quarry on many waters. Being a coarse fish, this species breeds six months earlier than the trout, so when the latter is uninterested in feeding and the flycatcher would normally be putting his rods away for the winter, the grayling is at its peak. Although the coarse fishing season extends through the winter, the hatches of fly are dependent on the warmer months; thus fishing for grayling is restricted to the autumn. Nevertheless, when a shoal is discovered, good sport may be had, for this species is an enthusiastic feeder which will rise repeatedly to the angler's fly. As the grayling shares the same waters as the trout, it is hardly surprising that most patterns suitable for the one will catch the other, but artificials which have a red tag or body are particularly effective.

The *Red Tag* (above), for example, is an important pattern to grayling but equally useful for trout. Tied by Martyn Flyn around 1850 and formerly called the Worcester Gem after its county of origin, it was introduced to Yorkshire grayling about thirty years later and proved so successful that it has been in use ever since. When tied with an orange tag, originally from the Indian crow, it is known as *Treacle Parkin* (centre).

Bearing a remarkable resemblance to both these patterns is *Terry's Terror* (right), a dry fly devised by Ernest Lock and Dr Cecil Terry for fishing the chalkstreams of southern England. In this case, however, goat's hair dyed yellow and orange forms the tag, and the peacock-herl body is ribbed with flat copper and gold tinsel. In its smaller sizes, as illustrated, Terry's Terror is reputed to be an effective iron blue pattern. Be that as it may, this size dressing is effective with grayling. Larger, longer shanked versions are fair representatives of caddis flies.

Sawyer Variants

awyer developed his Grayling Bug, later renamed *Killer Bug* (above) by an American visitor, for the selective culling of the species. It represents the freshwater shrimp, although to some it is more suggestive of a maggot, and was originally tied with a base of electrical fuse wire and a body of darning wool, a material more commonly associated with the mending of socks. Sawyer claimed that the colour – fawn with a pinkish tinge – was particularly important, and found that Chadwick's 477 wool, when wet, would closely match the hue of the shrimp's body. Unfortunately, Messrs Chadwick seemed oblivious to the ready market among anglers and discontinued their production many years ago, so the search for a perfect substitute has become a quest within a hobby. The fuse wire also seems to have been lost along the way, in favour of copper wire.

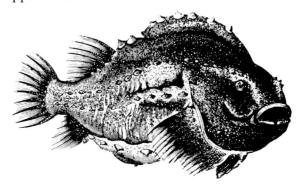

The *Bow Tie Buzzer* (centre) is a rather novel creation to imitate midge larvae. The body is ordinary enough, rather similar to the Pheasant Tail Nymph, but the fishing line was threaded through the hook and then tied around a piece of wool which served the dual role of representing breathing filaments whilst preventing the hook from sliding off. Unimpeded by attachment to the body of the pattern, the wool was free to spin and flutter, but later copies incorporated this feature in the pattern itself. Sawyer's nymph patterns were adopted and adapted in countless ways, although the originals remain as effective as ever. One form of embellishment is the *Green Variant* (below), a pattern tied with a fluorescent green thorax.

BASS

Leeches

British & American Variants

Leeches are common inhabitants of lakes and rivers, but whereas their imitation is largely ignored by river anglers, those fishing the stillwaters recognise leeches as a food form and tie patterns to mimic them, more so in the United States than in Britain.

The British have eleven species to imitate, varying in colour from black to brown, but close mimicry is disregarded in favour of a long black lure such as a Nobbler. It has been suggested that the *Black Tandem Lure* (above) was tied in imitation of a leech – it is certainly the correct size and shape – but in practice it is generally fished with a fast retrieve, and although the bottom-dwelling leech will move around quite a bit, swimming in a jerky, ungainly fashion, it certainly does not travel at the speeds attained by a lure stripped through the water. Besides, the popular embellishment of jungle-cock cheeks suggests that it is merely a general purpose lure, not representative of any special food form, and that the fish takes it only because it is guided by simple aggressive instincts.

Obviously it is a different story in North America where fishermen make a point of imitating the leech, as exemplified by the next two artificials. The fur bodies of the *Orange Leech* (centre) and the *Black Leech* (right) conceal an

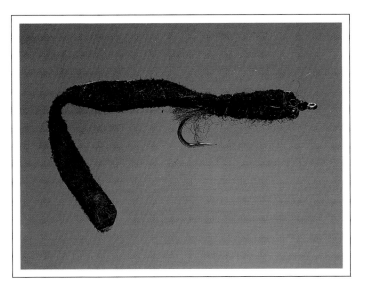

underbody of lead wire to ensure the pattern reaches the bottom, where the natural lives, and a strip of chamois leather, tied behind the eye and allowed to trail behind, imparts the desired movement.

Bass Bugs

When is a fly not a fly? None of the patterns illustrated on this page could be classified as artificial flies but they do represent legitimate food forms and are masterpieces of imitation. Mice and water voles may be taken by large trout – Bob Church found a deerhair vole imitation useful in the early days of Grafham Reservoir – but the patterns are ostensibly used to tempt the freshwater bass, a species not found in Britain but of immense importance to American anglers who pursue their sport in waters which abound in weed and sunken tree roots, a sufficient challenge to any fisherman.

The *Water Vole* (above) has a clipped deerhair body, leather patch ears, bead eyes and a strip of leather to produce a tough yet malleable tail. The *Lemming* (centre), looking more like a hedgehog than a suicidal rodent, uses a tuft of hair to create a bushier tail.

The *Frog* (below) is a good example of the fly-tyer's ingenuity in simulating this favourite item of the bass's diet. The eyes actually move and the legs are represented by bunches of knotted elastic, while the body colouring shows just how well deerhair accepts a dye. The loop of monofilament below the hook is a device to prevent the large hook from fouling surface weed, a method introduced to Britain by John Veniard in order to facilitate the use of large lures in difficult weedy waters; but the idea never became popular as most anglers believed the technique would adversely affect the pattern's hooking properties.

Zonkers

Not far removed from the New Zealand Matuka style is the Zonker series. Here again, the Zonker is a style of tying rather than a specific pattern, the feather wing of the Matuka being replaced by a strip of rabbit fur complete with hide. This strip is glued along the top of the hook before tying in at both tail and head. Whisks of the same colour as the winging material are standard – soft hen hackles provide the required mobility – together with a mylar tubing body.

The *Pearl Zonker* (above) is the original pattern and serves as a good fry imitator for both trout and bass. Bass fishing is very much an American pursuit – if the grayling may be called the fourth gamefish, the bass should perhaps be the fifth. Nevertheless, it is still used in Britain extensively as a fry imitator by stillwater anglers. As with any other successful lure, derivations have followed, including the *Green Zonker* (below). In this example, the properties of braided mylar have been employed to full effect, for the diameter of a braid increases when condensed along its length and decreases when stretched; push the two ends together and it gets wider, pull them and it becomes narrower. With this in mind, the dexterous tyer can closely imitate the taper of a fish. Although the soft rabbit fur is easy to obtain, the small strips required for this lure, aptly named Zonker strips, are commercially available – an indication both of the popularity and effectiveness of this pattern.

INDEX

Ace of Spades *101*
Adams *37, 42*
Adams Irresistible *37*
Adult Damselfly *64*
Al Troth's Terrible Stone *62*
Alder Fly *21*
Alexandra *58*
Amber Nymph *35*
Angler's Curse *see Caenis*
Ant *18*
ants 18, 37
Appetiser *99*
Austin, R.S. 40, 104

Baby Doll *106*
Bare Hook Nymph *46*
Barry Welham Nymph *74*
bass
  flies 121–5
Beacon Beige *35*
beetles 32, 86
Bell, Dr H.A. 35
Bergman, Ray 37
Bitch Creek *86*
Black and Peacock Spider *87*
Black Deerhair Beetle *86*
Black Doctor *113*
Black Dog Nobbler *98*
black flies 33
Black Gnat *33*
Black Hatching Buzzer *82*
Black Leech 122, *123*
Black Midge Pupa *80*
Black Muddler *100*
Black Spinner *43*
Black Tandem Lure *122*
Blae and Black *58*
Blagdon Buzzer 35
Blagdon Green Midge *82*
Blagdon Lake 35, 82, 91
Bloodworm *65*
Bloody Butcher *56*
Blue Doctor 113
Blue Upright *40*
Blue Zulu *54*
Blue-winged Olive *42*
Blue-winged Olive Dun *22*
bob flies 54
Bobby *97*
Bow Tie Buzzer *120*
Brock, Syd 95
Brown Collyer Nymph *74*
Brown Woolly *74*
Buff Chomper *83*
bumbles 55
Butcher *56*
Butcher series 56–7
buzzers 80–82

caddisflies *see* sedgeflies
Caenis 41
Caperer *36*
Caterpillar *18*
chompers 83
Christmas Tree *102*
Church Fry *90*
Church, Bob 90, 96, 99, 102, 124
Claret Bumble *55*
Clarke, Brian 103, 106
Coch-Y-Bonddhu *32*

Collyer, David 74, 101
Corixidae *see* water boatmen
Correll, George 28
Cotton, Charles 55
Cove's Pheasant Tail *70*
Cove, Arthur 70–71
craneflies *see* daddy-long-legs
Cream Spinner *43*

daddy-long-legs 19
damps 9
damselflies 64
dapping 76
Dark Last Hope *41*
Darker Twitchitt Nymph *75*
Darter *95*
Deane, Peter 35, 116
Deerhopper *20*
Demoiselle *64*
doctors 113
dog nobblers 96
Dogsbody *94*
dragonflies 64
drakes *see* mayflies
Drury, Lt-Col, Esmond 116
dry flies 9, 17–50, 66
Dry Greenwell *26*
Dry Iron Blue *50*
Dry March Brown *52*
Dulverton 35
Dunkeld *58*
Dunn, Captain J.J. 91
Durham Ranger *112*

Elk Hair Sedge *27*
Elver Fly *112*

Falkus, Hugh 108–9
feathers 11–12
  brown partridge *101*
  hackle *53*
  pheasant tail *71*
  rare 111–16
  teal breast *110*
February Red 53
fish
  instincts 10
Floating Fry *95*
Fluorescent Red Dad's Daddy *19*
fly-tying
  equipment 30
  history 7–8
  imitation factors 9–10
  methods 13, 15; *see also* under named flies
flyboxes 36
Flyn, Martyn 118
French Partridge Spent Mayfly *25*
Frog *124*
frog nobblers 96–7
fry 90–91, 95, 99
fry-bashing 89
fur 12–13

G & H Sedge *27*
Gapen, Don 100
Gary Dog *50*
General Practitioner *116*
Girdle Bug *86*
Glowstickle 89
Goddard, John 32, 41, 84
Gold-ribbed Hare's Ear *47*
Gold-ribbed Hare's Ear Nymph *47*

Golden Olive Bumble *55*
Gollidoll *106*
Goose Nymph *69*
Grasshopper *20*
Gray Ghost *102*
grayling
  flies 55, 117–20
Grayling Bug *see* Killer Bug
Green Chomper *83*
Green Collyer Nymph *74*
Green Corixa *72*
Green Drake *24*
Green Midge Pupa *81*
Green Partridge Mayfly *24*
Green Variant *120*
Green Zonker *125*
Green-and-Brown *87*
Greenwell, Canon William 26
Greenwell's Glory *26*
Grenadier *35*
Grey Duster *32*
Grey Wulff *44*
Grey Wulff Mayfly *45*
Grizzly Wulff *45*

Halford, Frederick 33, 34, 66
Halladay, Leonard 37
Hardy, J.J. 60
Hardy's Favourite *60*
Hardy's Gold Butcher *60*
Hatching Buzzer *82*
Hatching Midge Pupa *80*
Hawthorn Fly *18*
Honey Half Stone *40*
hooks 10
Houghton Ruby *36*
Houseby, Trevor 96

induced take technique 46
insects
  life cycles 8–9
Invicta *59*
Iron Blue Dun *50*
iron blues 50, 53
Irresistible series 37
Ivens, Tom C. 87

Jersey Herd *87*
Jewhurst and Moon 56
Jock Scott *114*

Kench, Brian 106
Killer Bug *120*
Kingfisher Butcher *56*
Kingsmill-Moore, T.C. 55
Kite, Major Oliver 12, 46
Kite's Imperial *46*

Lady of the Lake *see* Alexandra
Last Hope *41*
Latex Grub *33*
leeches 121–5
Lemming *124*
Lewis, Les 102
Little Red Sedge *34*
Lively Mayfly *24*
loch flies 58–60, 110
Lock, Ernest 119
lumphs 84
Lunn, William 36
Lunn's Particular *36*
lures 85–106

Mallard and Claret 59
Mar Lodge 114
Marabou Bloodworm 65
March Brown 42, 52
March Brown Nymph 52
Marinaro, Vincent 42
Marryat, Captain George 66
materials 10–11; see also under named flies
   storage 48
Matuka style 101
mayflies 24–5, 45, 63, 69, 88
Mayfly Nymph 63, 88
Medicine Fly 108
mice 124
midges 80–82, 120
Minister's Golden see Gary Dog
Missionary 91
Monofilament Daddy 19
Montana Nymph 84
Montana Variant 84
Moon's Fly see Butcher series
Mrs Palmer 88
Mrs Simpson 101
muddlers 100
Murdoch, William 59
Mylar Minnow 95

Nailer 98
Natural Daddy 19
nymphs 61–84

Ogden, James 47, 59
Olive Dog Nobbler 96
Olive Spinner 43
olives 22–3, 28, 42, 43, 104
Orange Chomper 83
Orange Leech 122
Orange Marabou Muddler 100
Orange Pheasant Tail Variant 70, 71
Orange Quill 34
Orvis Company 27, 84

palmering 54
Parachute Sedge 27
Parton, Steve 102
Partridge and Blue 53
Partridge and Orange 53
Patridge and Yellow 53
Peach Baby Doll 106
Pearl Zonker 125
Pearson, Alan 75
Persuader 84
Peter Ross 59
Pheasant Tail 23
Pheasant Tail Nymph 69
Plastazote Corixa 72
plastics 13, 63, 78–9
Polystickle 89
Powell, Harry 94
prawns 116
PVC Nymph 78

Ransome, Arthur 112
Red Hatching Buzzer 82
Red Tag 118
Red Wulff 44
Rough Olive 26
Royal Wulff 45

salmon 10
   flies 111–16
Sawyer, Frank 68–9

Secret Weapon 109
sedgeflies 27–9, 34, 36, 59, 87
Sherry Spinner 22
Shrimp 116
Shrimper 73
Shrine, Dick 91, 98
Silhouette Mayfly 25
Silver and Blue 55
Silver Corixa 72
Silver Doctor 113
Sinfoil, Ken 79
Sinfoil's Fry 79
Skues, G.E.M. 12, 15, 22, 28, 34, 62, 104
slips 59
smutting 28
Snipe and Purple 53
Snipe and Yellow 53
Soldier Palmer 54
Spent Black Drake 25
spinners 43
SS Nymph 68, 69
Stevens, Carrie 102
Stickfly 75
sticklebacks 89
Stillborn Mayfly 63
stoneflies 40, 62, 78
Stonefly Creeper 62
storage see flyboxes, materials
streamer patterns 102
Sunk Lure 108
Suspender Mayfly Nymph 63
Suspender Midge Pupa 80
Swannundaze Stonefly Larva 78
Sweeney Todd 94

Teal and Green 110
Teal, Blue and Silver 110
teal series 107–10
Ted's Stonefly 62
Terry, Dr Cecil 119
Terry's Terror 119
threads 92
Treacle Parkin 118
trout, river
   flies 17–106
trout, sea
   flies 107–10
Trueblood, Ted 62
Tup's Indispensable 104
Twitchfit Nymph 75

Undertaker, The 106

Venables, Colonel Richard 12
Veniard, John 101, 124
Viva 98
voles 124

Walker, Richard 88–9, 94
water boatmen 72
Water Vole 124
Watson's Fancy 60
Welshman's Button see Caperer
wet flies 9, 51–60
Whillock, Albert 90
Whisky Fly 90
White Chomper 83
White Irresistible 37
White Muddler 100
White Wulff 44
Whitlock, Dave 62
Wickham's Fancy 28

Wiggle Nymph 64
Willow Fly 62
Worcester Gem see Red Tag
Wright, James 26, 50, 112, 113
Wulff patterns 44–5
Wulff, Lee 44

Yellow Dog see Gary Dog
Yellow Francis 116
Yellow Sally 62
Yellow Torrish 115

zonkers 125
Zugbug 65
Zulu 54